Come Home!

Reclaiming Spirituality and Community as Gay Men and Lesbians

Chris Glaser

Chris Glaser (signature)

HARPER & ROW, PUBLISHERS, San Francisco

New York, Grand Rapids, Philadelphia, St. Louis

1817 London, Singapore, Sydney, Tokyo, Toronto

FIRST EDITION

Library of Congress Cataloging-in-Publication Data

Glaser, Chris.
　　Come home! : reclaiming spirituality and community
　　as gay men and lesbians / Chris Glaser.—1st ed.
　　　　p.　　cm.
　　ISBN 0-06-063124-4
　　1. Gays—Religious life.　2. Homosexuality—Religious aspects—Christianity.　I. Title.
　　BV4596.G38G57　　1990
　　208'.664—dc20　　　　　　　　　　　　　　　89-45958
　　　　　　　　　　　　　　　　　　　　　　　　　CIP

90　91　92　93　94　HAD　10　9　8　7　6　5　4　3　2　1

In thanksgiving to God
for those who have taught me so much about home:
my mother and father,
Mildred Cronister Glaser
and
Arthur Wayne Glaser,
and my lover,
George Franklin Lynch, Jr.

Contents

Acknowledgments

I thank God for the West Hollywood Presbyterian Church, the spiritual community in which I grew for ten years as Director of the Lazarus Project. It was there that many of the reflections in this book were born, tested, and modified. I thank God, too, for Presbyterians for Lesbian & Gay Concerns, a nationwide spiritual community to whose newsletter I've contributed many articles and columns. There, too, I was enabled to develop both writing skills and spiritual insights, insights that are not just mine, but that grow from our faithful experience together as gay, bisexual, and straight Christians.

Two continuing opportunities for retreat have contributed to my sense of perspective and meaning. One has been provided by the Order of the Holy Cross, whose Mount Calvary Retreat House in Santa Barbara proved a spiritual home-away-from-home. The other is a gift of a therapist, the Rev. Rick Thyne, who facilitated my awareness of the importance of "home" in my life.

Thanks to Yvonne Keller, my initial editor at Harper & Row, who helped me decide the form of this book. Thanks to Mel White and George Lynch for dragging me into the computer age with this manuscript. I thank my friends Pat Hoffman and David Jones for being my first readers and helpful critics. I thank Becky Laird for her editorial comments. Thanks go to copyeditor Linda Brubaker for helping me to be clearer in my writing. Finally, I am very grateful for editor

Jan Johnson's continuing encouragement and constructive suggestions regarding form and content.

I thank God for all who make a book like this possible, not the least of which are you the readers!

C. R. G.

Introduction

Softly and tenderly Jesus is calling,
Calling for you and for me;
Patient and loving, he's waiting and watching,
Watching for you and for me.
Come home, come home,
Ye who are weary, come home . . .

—HYMN BY WILL THOMPSON

Circumstances required me to make an unexpected and yet relaxing hour's drive to a relatively sleepy town called Orange. My mission was to obtain three hundred blank cassette tapes on which to record and duplicate the lectures of Dr. John Boswell, author of *Christianity, Social Tolerance, and Homosexuality.* I had no problem finding a parking space just beyond the town's single traffic circle and directly in front of the tape distributor. As I opened my car door, the pastor of the local Presbyterian church whizzed past in his sports car. This seemed like everyone's hometown, desired or real, a welcoming sanctuary in contrast to the seeming indifference of Los Angeles. Yet I remembered that some friends consider this area "behind the Orange Curtain" in reference to the conservative leanings of Orange County, home of the John Birch Society.

Entering the store, I found every indication that it was operated by Christians. A "Hear and Believe" tape cassette series prominently featured Dale Evans reading familiar biblical stories. A sign near the cash register read: "Yes, we extend credit . . . to God, who gives us the wisdom to ask for cash, check, or bank card." The man and the woman who handled my order for the church were gentle and kind. A wave of nostalgia came over me as I felt them treat me as a Christian brother, much as I had experienced at the hands of Christians in my youth before my politics and, later, my sexuality came into play in my relationship with the church.

I wondered what they would think if they knew the congregation I represented was largely gay in membership. I wondered if they would appreciate the insights about homosexuality and the church to be recorded on the tapes I purchased. The same audiotapes which contained Dale Evans' voice describing God's creation of a diverse world would also fix in magnetic memory John Boswell's revelations of gay saints, lesbian nuns, and a gay marriage ceremony, all from the Middle Ages. Would Jim, who now encouraged me to fill out an account application for further business, still be welcoming of future transactions if he knew?

On the drive home to West Hollywood, I pondered the fleeting feelings I enjoyed with this Christian brother and sister. First and foremost, I felt a sense of being home, a place where "they have to take you in," but also, a place where they *want* to take you in. In the ideal experience of it, home is a place for healing wounds and celebrating fulfillment. It's an environment which welcomes you to kick off your shoes, sink into an armchair, and put your feet up. You can be yourself. The masks are down, and you become as comfortable and vulnerable as a sleepy puppy. How I wished the church could be such a place for me! I thought of how many gay people needed just such a home within the family of faith.

Many lesbian women and gay men only know home as an ideal. Some of us suffered physical or emotional abuse growing up. Most of us experienced homophobic abuse. Because we did not feel welcome as we were, the masks came early: masking our feelings, overcoming our one "bad" trait by over-achieving socially, academically, athletically, spiritually, or aesthetically. Or perhaps we covered ourselves another way by becoming as bad or as irresponsible or as unattractive as we believed ourselves to be. That way no one would love us enough to discover our secret. Too many of us hid our difference by choosing death in its literal form or its figurative forms. To choose life usually meant leaving whatever home we had, often never to return.

Jesus made his home with the family of faith. "Foxes have holes, and birds have nests," he declared, "but the Human One has no place to lay his head" (Luke 9:58). Jesus knew what homelessness meant, figuratively and literally. When his mother and brothers and sisters came to see him, he responded, "Who are my mother and brothers and sisters? Those who do the will of my Father in heaven. They are my mother and brothers and sisters" (Mark 3:33–35). Jesus knew that his true family was more than biological; his true family were those who exercised the mercy and justice and love of God.

The family of faith has usually been less welcoming of Jesus' lesbian and gay relatives than their biological families have been. The church of our time has offered little sanctuary for homosexual orientation and expression. To "succeed" spiritually has required denial of our sexuality. It often also demanded suffering in silence, because the subject itself has been considered taboo. We could only hope that our "thorn in the flesh" would make us better Christians.

When gays and lesbians began affirming our gifts of love, we usually did so outside of religious institutions. Often we reflected back toward the church the rejection, the anger, and the hatred it had demonstrated toward us. But some of us did not. We remained within the church, becoming targets of the church's homophobia and of the gay community's churchphobia. Others of us found ourselves somewhere in between, not completely rejecting Christianity nor fully embracing it, but trying to integrate our spiritual and sexual feelings outside the Christian community.

Anyone who knows Jesus also knows this is not his wish for us. Jesus would not want us to be outside the family of faith, nor isolated within it. Jesus would be waiting at the church's doorway, welcoming us in before we tried to speak any words seeking his approval. Jesus would be knocking on the doors of the church's closets, inviting us to feel at home as we are. For Christians, Jesus' words and deeds reveal God's intent. To believe that Jesus would welcome us home is to believe that God welcomes us, not only into the family of faith, but the family of humankind.

This book is written for persons outside and within the church, as well as the many standing on the church's threshold. It is written for gays and lesbians, as well as others seeking to benefit from gay spirituality and ministry. It is an invitation to come home to Christian tradition and community. Like any homecoming, risk and vulnerability will accompany the joy and hospitality we experience. But the spiritual wealth of God's love and hope and peace awaiting us far exceeds the temporary and occasional poverty we may endure as we seek a new Christian reformation.

Every Christian community has heard Jesus' words and the words of scripture as if they applied to that particular community. Lesbian and gay Christians have frequently been denied that experience, often being so isolated from one another that we have been denied community among ourselves. For this reason, throughout this book I often quote or paraphrase scripture as if the author had the gay and lesbian Christian community in mind. Though exegetically problematic, I believe it is as justifiable to do so as it is to apply these words to any group of Christians outside the communities to which the biblical stories or letters were originally addressed. I believe that hearing the Bible as if addressed to us is part of the welcome home extended to us by God in Jesus Christ, *the* Word of God.

I will describe coming home to our spirituality in five spiritual movements. Though presented as if they were sequential and chronological, they may be experienced as coincidental or cyclical. Coming home to our spirituality begins with *accepting God's ways of welcoming* us (part I). Accepting God's embrace in returning home leads toward *receiving our spiritual inheritance* (part II). Having received the inheritance of our faith, we try to *discern what God calls us to do* with it (part III). Coming home to our spirituality and ministry entails interpretation: *making our witness* both to the church and to the lesbian and gay community (part IV). Finally, we *offer our unique vision* of God's inbreaking commonwealth (part V).

My hope is that readers will discern what is spiritually true for them as they read and welcome those truths into their evolving spirituality. I invite readers to wrestle with parts which don't seem to fit before ignoring or discarding them. And I ask that what is ignored or discarded may at least be tolerated within others, as we each develop our own spiritual/sexual configurations of integrity.

One of the greatest disagreements we must tolerate is whether or not these configurations include the institutional church. By nature, Christianity is a communal faith. But whether or not the community of believers to which one feels called to participate is a church or a support group or some other expression remains an individual choice. In making such a choice, we might consider the insight that mutual forgiveness is a desirable characteristic of home. No matter how divinely inspired, the church is a human institution. Like all human beings, it too needs forgiveness—God's and ours.

I don't quite understand why it is that, of all the homophobic institutions in which we participate daily, religious institutions are frequently the first we give up on. Perhaps it is simply because religion encourages an idealism about itself that is difficult to maintain in the face of prejudice, double standards, duplicity, and hypocrisy. Possibly it is because religious involvement is viewed as expendable in much of European and American society, so that lesbians and gays in those regions easily substitute other commitments. The family orientation that characterizes at least American religion certainly discourages the participation of single people and those individuals in nontraditional family patterns. But, in other parts of the world and some parts of American and European society, religion frequently plays a central, vital role that makes it less easy to abandon. Those of us who are freer to walk away from religion might consider the effect that such abandonment might have on lesbian sisters and gay brothers in the faith who do not see abandoning religion or religious institutions as options.

The Lazarus Project, which I directed for nearly a decade, is a ministry intended to welcome lesbian women and gay men home to their spirituality, their Christian faith, and the church. As Jesus called Lazarus back home to the life of his community, those who established the Project believed that Jesus was welcoming lesbians and gays back home to the life of Christian community. What was most important to us was that gays and lesbians recognize and value their spirituality as well as their sexuality. For those who also wished to learn of Christianity, worship and Bible study and spiritual counseling were available. The West Hollywood Presbyterian Church served as home for the Project and for many of the people who participated in the Project's ministry, either as the ministered or the ministers. Having learned what it meant to come home to the church, the Lazarus Project, under new leadership, now helps other congregations become more hospitable toward gay and lesbian Christians.

Regardless of resistance and resentment on the part of other Christians and despite our own temptations to stay away or remain closeted, fearful that we don't belong, I believe lesbian women and gay men are coming home to our spirituality. For many, the path does not return to their former religions. Some blaze trails toward less traditional or less familiar expressions of spirituality. A few follow a narrow road toward a freshly understood Christian faith, one informed by new knowledge, confidence, and self-esteem. Yes, like our heterosexual counterparts, we have sins to repent. But our homosexuality is not one of them.

What do gay and lesbian Christians stand to gain in coming home to our spirituality? Thousands of years of spiritual experience, first of the Hebrews and then of the Christians. Our own rights to the covenants of promise that God has made with humanity, from the rainbow to the cross. Our own gay history as shapers of the Christian community since its inception. Our own gay and lesbian communities of faith which are presently shaping the church. Our own spiritual power as Jesus' disciples and as members of the Body of Christ, infused with the Holy Spirit. And our dual citizenship in the community of believers and in the commonwealth of God. In all of these, we are as much recipients of God's grace and gifts as any other Christian. In our own times of crisis, whether experiencing gay-bashing, rejection, discrimination, or AIDS, we need all the spiritual resources we can get.

What does the broader Christian community stand to gain by welcoming us home? Our celebration of God-given sexuality as yet another means of God's grace. Our conscious working out of the relationship of sexuality and spirituality. Our keen sense of God's presence and love as we have experienced societal marginalization and disregard. Our valuing of personal experience in our spiritual journeys. Our ability in the face of spiritual and sexual ambiguities to make sexual and spiritual commitments. Our existential enjoyment of life, as well as our faith in life's continuity beyond death in the face of AIDS. These gifts and more will add to the church's spiritual resources and faith.

Only the Spirit may serve as guide for gays and lesbians finding their own way toward Christianity. At most, books such as this may serve as guideposts along the way. I invite those who are neither lesbian nor gay to come along, because lesbian and gay Christians have spiritual gifts to offer you. Together we may find "the wonderful love Jesus has promised, promised for you and for me."

Chris Glaser
West Hollywood, California

Come Home!

PART I

Welcoming God's Acceptance

The harmonizing of Gentiles and Jews within the early Christian church may serve as a paradigm for the harmonizing of persons of different sexual orientations in the present church. One of the apostle Paul's most spiritually uplifting writings, the letter to the Ephesians, addresses the relationship of Jewish and Gentile Christians. In doing so, I believe, he speaks to all diversity within the church: "For Christ is our peace, who has made us both one" (Eph. 2:14).

Many lesbians and gay men will understand from experience this description of the former alienation of Gentiles: "remember that you were at that time separated from Christ, alienated from the commonwealth of Israel, and strangers to the covenants of promise" (Eph. 2:12).

We might hear God's wish for us in these words: "that Christ may dwell in your hearts through faith; that you, being rooted and grounded in love, may have power to comprehend with all the saints what is the breadth and length and height and depth, and to know the love of Christ which surpasses knowledge, that you may be filled with all the fullness of God" (Eph. 3:17–19).

Once able to welcome God's acceptance of us as gays and lesbians, we can better hear Paul's description of reconciliation: "So then you are no longer strangers and sojourners, but you are fellow citizens with the saints and members of the household of God" (Eph. 2:19).

We have sometimes believed that one had to be extraordinarily good, wise, or powerful in *applying for sainthood* (chapter 1). But, amidst the din of the negative messages that the church and society give lesbians and gay men, we are *hearing God's yes* to us pronounced simply by virtue of our creation and our baptism (chapter 2). We do more than hear it, we feel it within our bodies, as we discover God's Word of love *welcoming embodiment* in Jesus and in us (chapter 3). Discerning what is spiritually true for us in the Bible requires a better *understanding of scripture* than most of us have been taught (chapter 4).

CHAPTER 1

Applying for Sainthood
(A Fantasy)

One Saint Patrick's Day, my contemplation of the life of this great Irish saint was interrupted by the entrance into my office of a tall, handsome stranger. His six-foot-two-inch frame, fleshed out in massive muscles, filled the doorway. He was blonde, with fair skin, and his perfect teeth caught whatever glint of sun entered my north-facing office. Well-spoken, his voice and manner harmoniously blended strength and gentleness. He was clothed stylishly in a Pierre Cardin blazer, Jordache slacks, and Gucci shoes. Self-confident, he sat comfortably in the chair opposite me without invitation. Recovering from both surprise and awe, I asked him what he wanted.

"I want to apply for sainthood," he answered. I glanced outside in the church courtyard to see if my congregation had posted any "Help Wanted" signs. Seeing none, I was relieved. My own job was at least temporarily secure.

"What are your qualifications?" I inquired.

"I am good, wise, and have magical powers," he replied.

"Oh," I said, sarcasm creeping into my voice as I searched for a halo above his head. Facetiously, I asked, "How good are you?"

He became specific: "I have never taken God's name in vain; I've kept the Sabbath day holy; I honor my father and mother; I have never killed, committed adultery, stolen, nor coveted."

"Ever cheated on your income tax?" I countered.

"Never!" he said, not thrown off guard.

"Gone too far on a first date?" I pressed.

"Never! Most complain I don't go far enough!" came the response.

"Oh," I said. What was I to say? Here was a morally perfect person sitting before me, seemingly untainted by original sin or even second-hand sin. He was a male Mary Poppins, "practically perfect in every way."

"You mentioned you were wise?" I said in a questioning way, indicating I wanted examples.

"Yes," he said. "I am so wise that the president asked me to develop a peace plan for the Middle East."

"But you didn't!" I pointed out triumphantly, thinking this fellow had delusions of grandeur.

"I was wise enough to turn him down," he answered. I couldn't argue: that surely was the wiser choice!

"Well, what magical powers do you have? Can you show me a sign?" I asked, believing this might get him out of my office so I could resume my contemplation.

"Lend me a dollar," he said. As he departed with my dollar, I smiled, thinking to myself, "Just as I thought, he's just another panhandler looking for spare change." And I resumed my reflection on Saint Patrick.

But, within an hour's time, he returned, accompanied by a Brink's truck. "What's this?" I asked, surprised. What else could I be but surprised?

"Thank you. Here's your dollar back." Then he explained nonchalantly, "I invested your dollar and profited a million dollars within sixty minutes. It's in the truck. Want to count it?" The truck's doors were opened, and I discovered it stuffed with neatly stacked bills. "That's power," I confessed, confused. This was no ordinary Mary Poppins.

"Do I qualify for sainthood?" he queried.

"I'm not sure," I said, still hesitating. He was everything he said he was, but there was something missing. Not sure what it was, I considered the thought that perhaps the only thing missing was my sanity.

"Would you mind going for a drink?" I asked him, believing this delaying tactic would give me a chance to think.

"Not at all," he responded politely. "My treat."

My presence of mind must have been affected by the events of the day because, without considering the consequences, I took this stylish, wholesome man to a neighborhood Levi and leather bar called the Spike. The dark interior of the bar did not hide from my eyes my guest's blush at the sight of gay men in provocative clothing, from torn jeans to leather chaps. His presence had its effect on them as well, some smirking at his designer clothing. "Beverly Hills is that way!" one patron mocked, pointing toward the exit. Others ignored his clothes, visually stripping him naked as they looked lustfully at his healthy, well-developed body. He, in turn, sensing this, was embarrassed that he was causing men to sin in thought, if not in deed.

I ordered a beer; he ordered Perrier. "It figures," I thought. We roamed to the patio flooded with daylight and perched ourselves on a ledge along the wall. The sun seemed to shine a little more brightly on my new acquaintance. In the shadows at the back bar I noticed Sammy, who is half Polish and half Puerto Rican. Months ago, I found myself informally counseling him here. The poor guy felt like a mongrel, not accepted by his Polish relatives and ostracized by those from Puerto Rico. Far from his island home, he was an alien in many senses of the term. He was insecure, flighty, and undependable. He'd gone through five lovers, and was now being kept by a man who did not love him. He thirsted for affection, for affirmation, for some mission in his life. The gin and tonics he drank too often would never quench that thirst, and the alcohol blinded him to his deeper needs, not to mention making those needs obscure to those around him.

Now you should understand that I am not given to visions. Nor have I ever claimed to see Jesus Christ before. But, so help me, at that moment, Jesus Christ walked in the door. Jesus looked about, and I wondered if he might come and speak with me. Then I realized that, no, he'd probably seek out the good, wise, powerful, and handsome man beside me.

Instead, he sat next to Sammy, and said, "Buy me a drink." The man interested in sainthood, who also recognized Jesus, looked at me. We exchanged expressions of amazement.

Sammy seemed surprised, too. "Why would you ask a guy like me for a drink?" he asked.

Jesus answered, "If you knew God's gift to you, and if you knew who I am, you'd ask for a drink that would satisfy you forever."

Sammy, a little too drunk to follow, protested, "Hey man, you don't seem to be carrying a wallet, and drinks cost money; where would you get such a drink? Are you greater than this bartender?"

Jesus said to him, "Everybody who drinks these drinks will thirst again, but whoever drinks what I offer will become a wellspring for others."

Sammy replied, "Please, give me this drink so I won't be so thirsty, and I won't waste so much time here!"

"Go get your lover and come back here."

Sammy answered sadly, "I don't really have a lover."

"I know. You've had five lovers, and the one you're with doesn't truly love you."

"I guess you're some kind of mystic." Then Sammy felt obliged to make excuses: "I used to believe in all that stuff, y'know, spiritual things, God, and church—but I'm not particularly religious anymore. I didn't feel welcome in my church, being gay. So, Sundays I read the paper, go to brunch with friends, and hit the afternoon beer busts at the bars. I still pray sometimes, though, right here in the bar!"

Jesus told him, "Sammy, believe me, the time is coming—in fact, it's here right now—when whether you worship God on this bar stool or in church makes no difference. But you're unclear who or how you're worshiping right now. True worshipers will worship God in spirit and in truth. That's what God is looking for."

Sammy answered, "I know some messiah will come along and save me. I just haven't found the right man yet."

Jesus said, "You've found him now!"

We marveled that, of all people, Jesus would speak to Sammy, but we didn't say anything. Sammy left his drink and went up to others in the bar, saying, "Come on, meet someone who seems to understand what I need. Could this be the one I've been waiting for?" Some of these joined the circle growing around Jesus, and seemed to enjoy talking with him for a little while.

"See all you saints later!" Jesus shouted jovially as he departed.

"Well, I *never!*" exclaimed the would-be saint, resentful and disgusted. He abruptly left by the bar's back exit, slamming the door behind him. Dazed, I returned to my office.

There was something familiar about the scene I'd witnessed. Searching the scriptures, I realized why. The Gospel of John describes Jesus meeting the Samaritan woman at the well. She was a woman, rather disreputable, and from a so-called mongrel race known as Samaritans. Nonetheless, Jesus chose not only to speak with her, but also to reveal his messianic identity to her, transforming her into an evangelist in her Samaritan ghetto. She was not good, nor particularly wise, and certainly not powerful, yet Jesus called her to bring others into communion with him.

I thought about Saint Patrick. Behind legends, the truth is that Patrick as an English youth was kidnapped and enslaved by the Irish. He escaped his captors after six years, but felt called to carry the Gospel to his former oppressors in Ireland. The pope at first rejected his request to serve God in that capacity because of some unnamed sin of Patrick's youth. The pope sent someone else instead. But when that first missionary died, Patrick received the pope's blessing. Within a short time, he Christianized the entire nation of Ireland, becoming responsible for the founding of over one hundred churches with one hundred thousand converts.

Patrick had sinned, had no particular wisdom to set him apart from other priests, and had certainly experienced powerlessness during his enslavement. Yet he was called to be a missionary on behalf of Jesus Christ and was later canonized as a saint by the Roman Catholic Church for his efforts.

We Protestants believe in the priesthood of all believers, and we believe that Jesus Christ calls all believers saints: not necessarily perfect, wise, nor powerful, but saints nonetheless. Paul wrote: "For consider your call, brothers and sisters; not many of you were wise according to worldly standards, not many were powerful, not many were of noble birth: but God chose what is foolish in the world to shame the wise, God chose what is weak in the world to shame the strong, God chose what is low and despised in the world . . . so that no human being might boast in the presence of God" (1 Cor. 1:26–29).

With the Samaritan woman, we are called in our imperfection to spread the good news of God's love in Christ to our lesbian and gay community. With Saint Patrick, we are called in our weakness to convert even our oppressors to God's inclusive love. God's grace, God's unmerited mercy and favor, accepts us as we are. Though not perfect, nor necessarily wise, nor especially powerful, God's grace will enable us to fulfill our calling as saints.

By the way, if anyone is interested in purchasing a secondhand Pierre Cardin blazer, size 42, please drop me a line.

CHAPTER 2

Hearing God's Yes

Someone at the bar asks for your phone number. But you never get a call. You hear a yes and a no.

You hurt a friend's feelings. You sincerely apologize. She says she forgives you, but deep down you sense she is going to hold this over your head like the sword of Damocles. You hear a yes and a no.

The doctor seems encouraging about your response to treatment, yet seems hesitant to offer any prognosis. You hear a yes and a no.

You're trying to arrange a get-together with a friend. He keeps responding, "Yes, we've got to get together!" But he never seems to be available. You hear a yes and a no.

Your company boasts a nondiscrimination policy regarding gays and lesbians. But you notice no lesbian or gay man is promoted above a certain level. You hear a yes and a no.

Your family seems supportive following your coming out to them. However, they never invite your lover to family gatherings. You hear a yes and a no.

You and your lover have been considering living together. Your lover speaks of it dreamily, in romantic moments. But when you try to discuss concrete plans, such as "Should I renew my lease?" or "Do you mind living with cats?" the subject is changed. You hear a yes and a no.

"Do I make my plans like a worldly person, ready to say Yes and No at once?" the apostle Paul rhetorically wrote to the church at Corinth (2 Cor. 1:17).

We are surrounded by worldly persons, ready to say yes and no at once, from lover, family, and friends, to store clerks, church leaders, and politicians. We grow tired, frustrated, angry, and hurt by the constant string of double messages from people we think we know, as well as from strangers we don't know at all.

We don't want to hear yes and no. No is sometimes easier to take than a double message. But we prefer to hear Yes!

My sister was teaching her young son to say "please." He asked for a glass of milk, and my sister, fishing for "please," hinted, "What's the magic word?" "Yes?" he guessed.

Yes is the magic word. That is the word we wish to hear, whether asking for a glass of milk or for affirmation.

"Do I make my plans like a worldly person, ready to say Yes and No at once?" Paul wrote. "As surely as God is faithful, our word to you has not been Yes and No."

Paul intended to visit the Corinthian church, but had changed his plans. In this letter, Paul responds to charges that he is vacillating, undependable, and unreliable. He still plans to visit, but he's been rerouted and delayed.

Perhaps the Corinthian church members were a bit sensitive. They were a minority sect organizing a new community. They had no doubt been neglected, disappointed, and let down before. The worldly, majority culture could not be trusted. This made them all the more demanding of their own. And now even Paul—who had founded their church and written them an exalting letter on love and faith (1 Corinthians)—seemed to be letting them down. Was he making plans like a worldly person, ready to say yes and no at once?

Paul uses the occasion of their distrust to speak of God's faithfulness, of God's faithful yes spoken in Jesus Christ: "For the Child of God, Jesus Christ, was not Yes and No; but in Christ it is always yes. For all the promises of God find their Yes in Christ."

The "Yes in Christ," the good news of God's gracious love toward us all, has been shrouded for lesbians and gays by the church. The church has behaved like a worldly institution, ready to say yes and no at once to us. Yes, God loves you. But no, God doesn't love your sexuality. Yes, we love you, but only as long as you don't love someone of your own gender intimately. Yes, you may be members. No, you may not be ordained as leaders. Yes, we welcome your gifts of time, talent, and money. But no, we can't affirm your min-istries with ordination. Yes, we are concerned for the pain this causes you. But no, we won't bear the pain that affirming you will cause the church.

During the past fifteen years, I have spiritually counseled thousands of lesbian women and gay men. I have discovered that most of them needed to struggle with the noes pro-nounced against homosexuality in scripture, tradition, and present church policies. I would place in perspective the handful of scriptural admonitions against it. I would tell them of periods of church history in which homosexuality was bet-ter tolerated. I would explain that current church policy has been formulated precisely because the traditional wisdom on homosexuality is being questioned. Finally, to cut through to the heart of the matter, I would ask each one, "If Jesus were here right now, how do you think he would respond to you?" Invariably, uncoached, the response has been some variation of: "I think Jesus would hug me."

No matter how much the church has conditionalized God's love for gay and lesbian Christians, God's "Yes in Christ" graciously bursts forth, wrapping divine arms around us, wel-coming us home. Lesbian and gay Christians are hearing the "Yes in Christ." It is empowering us to challenge the worldly ambivalence of the institutional church. It is calling us into new communities of believers, from the Universal Fellowship of Metropolitan Community Churches to denominational caucuses. It is inspiring us to come home to our spirituality.

The "Yes in Christ" overpowers the noes of life. It overcomes the blindness of the self-righteous with new vision. It quickens those paralyzed by legalism so that they may go forward. It brings new life to a church community divided by its isolation of gay and lesbian members in closet-tombs. More miraculous than overcoming physical blindness, paralysis, and death, Jesus Christ's ministry overcomes doctrinal blindness, spiritual paralysis, and communal alienation. "Repent, for the kingdom of heaven is at hand!" Jesus preached. It is a call to turn from the noes of life to share in a common wealth of grace and love under the sovereignty of God. It becomes a form of vitality and empowerment, especially for the dispossessed, who need to hear that message all the more.

Yet the church throughout the ages and in this present time has revealed a worldly ambivalence toward this invitation. Being worldly persons, Christians have responded yes and no at once. Having a need for rules, the church has attempted to limit God's grace. Despite so much Christian selflessness, the church has often become selfish and parochial with God's love. The church has said yes and no to God by saying yes and no to strangers, neighbors, and fellow believers.

The apostle Paul, who could so boldly proclaim the "Yes in Christ," was no stranger to the church's mixed feelings. As Saul, blinded by religious doctrine, paralyzed from embracing God in Christ, he zealously imprisoned early Christians, alienating the small, Jewish sect from mainstream Judaism. On the road to Damascus, he met the yes in Christ. Forever transformed, renamed Paul, he preached what he had persecuted: God's "Yes in Christ." Not surprisingly, the early church looked warily on this feared and hated newcomer to the faith. Paul didn't get his ministry to the Gentiles approved by the church until fourteen years after the fact. He writes in his epistle to the Galatians, "When the one who had set me apart . . . was pleased to reveal the Son to me, in order that I might preach him among the Gentiles, I did not confer with flesh and blood, nor did I go up to Jerusalem to those who were apostles before me" (Gal. 1:15–17).

Then Paul writes, reflecting on his eventual approval by the authorities of the church, his "ordination": "And those who were reputed to be something . . . added nothing to me; but on the contrary, when they saw that I had been entrusted with the gospel to the uncircumcised [the Gentiles] just as Peter had been entrusted with the gospel to the circumcised [the Jews], and when they perceived the grace that was given to me, James and Peter and John, who were reputed to be pillars, gave to me the right hand of fellowship, that we should go to the Gentiles and they to the Jews" (Gal. 2: 6–9).

Paul's ministry was validated when the church perceived God's grace given to him and recognized his unique call to preach the gospel to the Gentiles. But Paul's ministry had begun fourteen years earlier, when he experienced God's grace and heard God's call.

Blinded by religious doctrine about homosexuality, paralyzed from embracing God in Christ because we did not feel worthy, many of us who are homosexual imprisoned our sexuality in a closet, experiencing alienation from our Christian home as well as from ourselves. On our road to spiritual integrity, we met the "Yes in Christ." Forever transformed, renamed gay or lesbian, we preach what we had rejected: God's "Yes in Christ" to us as homosexual women and men. Not surprisingly, the church looks warily on us as feared and hated members of the Christian family. But our ministry with our brothers and sisters, both gay and nongay, both Christian and non-Christian, already begins. Our ministry commences as we come home to our spirituality, as we hear the "Yes in

Christ" as lesbian and gay Christians. The church's validation of ourselves and our ministries is yet to come.

As I was driving out of a parking lot, the attendant stopped
me. "Have you been validated?" she asked. I thought a moment. "Not at the bar last night," I wanted to reply, "nor
recently by the church."

Of course she was asking if my parking ticket had been
validated. But the way she put her question allowed me to
consider the worldly ambivalence which we as gays and lesbians meet in our everyday lives, from bars to churches. I
tried to remember the last time I felt validated as a person.

To validate means to "mark with an indication of official
sanction." The biblical story of creation tells us that we are
validated simply by God's choosing to create us and give us
life. Scriptural heterosexism and heterosexist interpretations
would have us believe that homosexuality and homosexual
persons were not created by God. But now scientific studies
reveal that sexual orientation—whether heterosexual, homosexual, or bisexual—is sealed in the womb or in the early
years of life, long before conscious choice. To the person of
faith, this creation of sexual orientation is God's activity.
Having created us homosexual, it's not likely God would
abandon us now any more than God would abandon Gentiles, people of color, or women, all of whom were once
considered as less than fully made in the image of God.

And the biblical story of redemption tells us that we are
validated even when we fail to live up to our human potential, made in God's image. We are validated by God's grace
embodied in the forgiving love of Jesus Christ. This is the
empowering "Yes in Christ" of which Paul wrote to the Corinthians. It is into this yes that we are baptized.

So, if a parking authority should ask us, "Have you been
validated?" we can reply, "Yes, by creation and redemption."
That is ultimately our most important validation for parking
on this earth.

Though our existence is validated by creation and redemption, we know that the ways we express who we are or how we have been redeemed are not always validated, marked with an indication of official sanction.

Many times I have been asked by well-wishers, "When are they going to ordain you?" In other words, when is the church going to mark my ministry as a gay man with an indication of official sanction? I would take the question further: when is the church going to mark the ministries of all lesbian and gay Christians with an indication of official sanction? Remembering the apostle Paul's long wait for validation should encourage us.

Gay and lesbian Christians have been entrusted with a prophetic and pastoral ministry, preaching the gospel to gay and straight alike. We have met the "Yes in Christ." In the face of the church's worldly ambivalence, its ability to say yes and no at once to us, our accepting the "Yes in Christ" empowers us to perform our ministry in spite of the church. We do not seek validation for ourselves as children of God. By creation and redemption, we have already been validated as God's daughters and sons. We do urge the church to celebrate our validation with us by blessing our relationships and our ministries with "indications of official sanction": ceremonies of holy union and services of ordination.

Have gay and lesbian Christians been validated? By God, *Yes!* "For in Christ Jesus it is always Yes" (2 Cor. 1:19).

CHAPTER 3

Welcoming
Embodiment

A heterosexual woman deeply involved in the
ministry of the Lazarus Project once told us one of the reasons
for her commitment: from gay and lesbian Christians, she
experienced an "unconditional, positive regard." A heterosexual pastor echoed this at the end of one of our conferences
bringing gay and nongay together: "I feel like I can be myself
whenever I'm with all of you, saying what I really feel and
affirming what I really believe. I wish I could do the same in
my own congregation."

Through God's grace, we had somehow embodied for them
the "Yes in Christ." I believe that was possible because, also
through God's grace, we had experienced the "Yes in Christ"
in a congregation that made us feel at home. We had been
fed spiritually, hearing God's Word of love for us, feeding on
God's Word of love in our hearts.

God's Word of love is the "Yes in Christ" of which Paul
wrote: "For all the promises of God find their Yes in Christ"
(2 Cor. 1:20). The gospel writer John affirmed, "God's Word
became flesh" (John 1:14). Later, Jesus says, "For my flesh is
food indeed, and my blood is drink indeed" (John 6:55).

What a miracle to make God's Word of love flesh! How
we struggle to embody God's love for the world, whether with
friend, lover, or stranger, whether within church or commu-

nity. To even begin to embody God's love for the world, we need to be fed with Christ's body. We need to be fed with the embodiment of God's love for us. Ideas, philosophies, theologies of love are not satisfying enough. Reading theology is like reading pornography: instructive, provocative, but always pale in comparison to the real encounter. In Jesus Christ, we encounter God's love in the flesh. He offers us his body.

Once when I was feeling unloved, someone I loved offered me his body. We made love into the night, sleeping together in affectionate embrace. The next day, I felt loved, I believed in myself as lovable, I wanted to be loving—even to those who had proven unloving toward me. And I realized that God's love had become flesh once again. I understood sexuality as a means of grace, a way in which God lets us know how much God loves us, how intimately God loves us.

In the epilogue of my book *Uncommon Calling*, I wrote of a lesbian who came to a workshop on the church and homosexuality. Stating that she had no religious background, she explained that she had discovered in her lovemaking with her lover a spiritual realm. She said simply, "Since spirituality has to do with God, I came here to find out about God."

Sexuality is a means of grace, a way in which God's love may be embodied for us and within us. Deep within us, I believe, is a yearning for such embodied love: a hungry baby crying to be fed at her mother's breast; a fearful and restless infant needful of the secure, regular motion of father rocking him to sleep; a hurting child eager to crawl up on mommy or daddy's lap to make it better.

But as grownups, to whom do we turn when we're hungry? To whom do we turn when we're fearful and restless? To whom do we turn when we're hurting?

Like the beloved disciple Mary, hungry for Jesus' words, we might want to listen at his feet. Like the beloved disciple John, we might want to lean our troubled heads on Jesus' breast. Like the many who found healing for their illnesses or pain, we might hope for Jesus' touch.

But as we offer to wash Jesus' feet, as we begin to lean our heads on his breast, and as we reach to touch even the hem of his garment, self-righteous Pharisees have blocked us, saying, "Jesus doesn't associate with the likes of you! Go away! Get out of here! You are unclean, unwanted, you don't belong with us!"

Perhaps we ran home to mommy or daddy to kiss it and make it better only to find we can't go home again.

And so, many of us moved to the cities, places of anonymity which allowed us to be ourselves—lesbian, gay—but also places of isolation not necessarily conducive toward getting our needs met: our need for nurture, our need for security, our need for healing. Sometimes, living in the urban sprawl contributed to, rather than alleviated, our hunger, our fear, and our hurt.

Denied access to other ways in which God loves us, denied access to other means of grace, such as the church or our families, we relied more heavily upon our sexuality or involvement in the gay or women's community as ways of feeling loved, believing ourselves lovable, and offering love.

Many of us came of age in a love-starved, bruised, and abused gay ghetto, and it was difficult not to grow jaded, cynical, detached, and care-less as we searched for love's embodiments.

It's a miracle we survived. And it's a miracle our love survived. But our love is what made us survive. Our love became our food and drink when denied family meals or the eucharistic meal. Our love made us unique, helped us feel loved, called us into community, created home for us, which in turn increased our self-esteem, our valuing of ourselves and our love. The love that arose from our sexuality and our sexual communities became our means of grace, our embodiment of God's love for us, an incarnation of God's word of love for us.

Because of our age or our appearance, some of us received more love than others, some of us received less, some of us received none, and some of us rejected what love we got because of the age or appearance of the giver. More so among lesbians than gay men, ideology also factored into the giving and receiving of love. Long before AIDS hampered sexual intimacy and expanded our spiritual intimacy, gay and lesbian Christians knew that our sexuality alone could not adequately express the love within us. We knew our love was too often conditional. It wasn't always the "unconditional positive regard" one might associate with home.

"For my flesh is food indeed, and my blood is drink indeed. Those who eat of my flesh and drink of my blood, abide in me, and I in them" (John 6:55–56).

Something, someone lived in lesbian and gay Christians that was flesh and blood and yet more than flesh and blood: God's Word. God's Word of love for us all. God's Word of love for the stranger, the enemy, the unattractive. God's Word of love for all peoples, all creation. We had eaten of the flesh, we had drunk of the blood, of God's Word of love. Its denial by a less than gracious church had made us hungry for justice, restless for our spiritual homes, hurting for our sisters and brothers who suffer loss of love, loss of rights, loss of life.

"For my flesh is food indeed, and my blood is drink indeed. Those who eat of my flesh and drink of my blood abide in me, and I in them. As the living God sent me, and I live because of God, so whoever partakes of me will live because of me" (John 6:55–57).

What did Jesus know about living? When I was trying to come to terms with my own sexuality, I once complained to an elderly pastor, "It's hard for me to identify with Jesus, because he doesn't seem to have any sexuality." The pastor responded with his own difficulty identifying with Jesus because, as he said, "Jesus never had to face old age."

Kazantzakis' book *The Last Temptation of Christ* helped me to understand a Christ who struggled with his sexuality as well as his call to ministry, a struggle largely left out of the gospels. But we do catch other glimpses of Jesus' humanity: his temptations in the wilderness, his tears in the face of Lazarus' death, his delight in the woman who anointed his feet with ointment, his special love for the disciple John, his agony in the garden of Gethsemane. What did Jesus know about living? Exactly what we know: temptations, tears, delight, love, agony. And he knew something more: "I live because of God." And more: "Whoever partakes of me will live because of me."

I believe this means that whoever receives Jesus into her or his spirituality will choose the life God intends, as Jesus himself did. Whoever partakes of Jesus will both find and offer a spiritual home. Whoever partakes of Jesus will receive and extend a healing touch. Whoever partakes of Jesus will enjoy and be empowered to work for a merciful justice. Blessed are those restless for home, whose wounds need healing, and who seek justice, for they shall be satisfied. "Whoever partakes of me will live because of me."

In the gay men's community, we enjoyed sexuality as a means of grace. Then AIDS struck. Some have allowed it to reinforce a negativity about their sexuality. Some have allowed it to bolster their own fears of intimacy. Some have used it as an excuse to stop loving, to become isolated, to despair. But for most of us within the gay as well as the lesbian community, the true message of AIDS is that it makes us aware that we are intimately bound together, not by infection, but by a deep and abiding affection. Though AIDS physically struck gay men, both gays and lesbians have been emotionally and spiritually affected. And both have come to the support of their brothers with AIDS.

Several years ago, a church group attended an annual "supermen" contest. I attended reluctantly, because, though I enjoy looking at men's bodies, I have reservations about competitions based largely upon appearance. As I viewed one muscled, well-proportioned body after another, my mind kept returning to the emaciated, sore-covered body, struggling for breath, of a man suffering the final stages of AIDS, with whom and with whose family I had spent that very afternoon. I felt extremely close to him, his family, his friends. As almost everyone does who is personally affected by the AIDS crisis, I understood that we as a community are bound intimately together neither by an infection, nor by a superficial attraction, but by an affection that grows out of our welcoming embodiment.

AIDS has made us aware, if we did not realize it already, of how our appreciation of sexuality has expanded our capacity for nurturing, holding, and healing as we care for lovers, friends, neighbors, and strangers. AIDS also has made us aware, now more than ever, of the limitations of sexuality, the limitations of our bodies as we know them, as means of grace.

In our caregiving with persons with AIDS or ARC, in our coping with either HIV infection or an AIDS diagnosis, in our fearing HIV infection or the intimacy which may occasion it, we too need nurturing, holding, and healing. We too need to feed at mother's breast, be comforted in father's arms, have our wounds kissed. We too need home.

Our sexuality is a means of such grace, but it does not stand alone. "For my flesh is food indeed, and my blood is drink indeed. Those who eat of my flesh and drink of my blood abide in me, and I in them. As the living God sent me, and I live because of God, so whoever partakes of me will live because of me. This is the bread which came down from heaven, not such as our ancestors ate and died; whoever eats this bread will live for ever" (John 6:55–58). Jesus contrasts the manna God gave the Israelites in the wilderness with himself, the spiritual food God offers now. The manna appeared each morning and met daily needs. Jesus is always with us and meets eternal concerns. Both are equally vital to life. Neither is dispensable for the abundant life of the body.

Similarly, sexuality became our manna in the wilderness of rejection. It appeared as gracious gift and met our needs for embodied love. But sexuality is not our only means of nurturing. Spirituality must go hand in hand with our sexuality. Both are equally vital to life. Neither is dispensable for the abundant life of the body. We must be fed spiritually at Jesus' feet, lean our troubled heads on Jesus' breast, allow him to touch our wounded bodies.

One Saturday morning, I sat on the floor, reading. I wanted to be closer to Mother Earth than sitting on the sofa allowed. I had just read various newspaper articles about the controversy over the film *The Last Temptation of Christ*. One observer commented that the furor centered on the portrayal of Christ as sexual. Now I read a book entitled *WomanChrist*, by Christin Lore Weber, in which, as other feminist theologians have suggested, women's theology is described as arising from the body, body rhythms linking us to cosmic rhythms. I cried tears of recognition, realizing I too knew God partly through my own body. Outside the window, I could hear the voices of two neighbor girls, whose family had escaped the political brutality of Guatemala. One derided her sister saying, "You're black and ugly!" and making her cry. A little later I received a phone call from an older friend, reminding me of her body's struggle with cancer, although she expressed concern less for her own death than for the son she would leave behind in the midst of the AIDS crisis.

In that single hour, in those few events, I was reminded of how embodiment affects our spirituality. The film reminded me of the controversy over relating sexuality to spirituality. The book reminded me of the need to allow embodiment to shape our understanding of spirituality. When the little girl said, "You're black and ugly!" I was reminded of the oppression we inflict on one another by brutalities against the body in political conflict such as Guatemala suffers, or by rejection of different embodiments in personal conflict. And the conversation with my friend with cancer reminded me how love both inspires and transcends embodiment as we struggle against life-threatening illness, yet care for the welfare of our loved ones as we pass beyond the threshold of death.

"Whoever partakes of me will live because of me." There are those Christians who do not want to partake of Christ's body. There are those who want to disembody Christ. They want to make him asexual. They want to ignore his earthy concern for the well-being of the bodies of others. They want to harden their hearts against his suffering with victims of political violence, against his call to give up prejudice based on differences of embodiment, whether of color, age, sexual orientation, gender, or disability. They want to gloss over his own agony facing death.

These who want to disembody Christ today have a lot in common with those who wished to disembody Christ in the past, those who shouted, "Crucify him! Crucify him!"

Among those who want to crucify the body of Christ are those who want to crucify the body, period. They want to inhibit the body's sexuality. They want to ignore the body's needs. They want to forget bodily oppression. They want to discriminate based on embodiment. And they want to destroy the bodies of prophets who say things like: "For my flesh is food indeed, and my blood is drink indeed"—God's Word of love made flesh. In Jesus Christ, God welcomes the Word's embodiment.

"Those who eat of my flesh and drink of my blood abide in me, and I in them." Our call is to embody God's Word of love. In Jesus Christ, we are enabled to welcome the embodiments of others.

"Whoever partakes of me will live because of me." Then we'll know what life is really about. Those who want to crucify the body are those who would prevent us from sitting at Jesus' feet, leaning our faces on his breast, letting his hands caress us. But that's what life's about: feeding on mother God's breast, secure in father God's arms, healed and held by God. In Jesus Christ, God welcomes our embodiment.

"Whoever eats this bread will live for ever."

"Many of the disciples, when they heard it, said, 'This is a hard saying, who can listen to it?' But Jesus, knowing that the disciples murmured at it, said to them, 'Do you take offense at this?' . . . After this many of the disciples drew back and no longer went about with him. Jesus said to the twelve, 'Do you also wish to go away?' Simon Peter answered Jesus, 'To whom shall we go? You have the words of eternal life; and we have believed, and have come to know, that you are the Holy One of God'" (John 6:60–61, 66–69).

CHAPTER 4

Understanding Scripture

In the process of discerning spiritual truths, readers of the Bible both within and outside the church often inadequately understand scripture. Such misinterpretations, caused by everything from "innocent" ignorance to wanton prejudice, sometimes inflict unnecessary grief and pain. They do a disservice to the integrity of scripture, because they usually fail to reflect the Bible's broadest themes. Often they are employed by those who are jealous of the permissiveness of God's grace, fearful of freedom for themselves, and eager to keep sisters and brothers in line. This is too often true in the church; ironically, I witness the phenomenon as frequently among those not strongly identified with the church, the so-called secularized, who will say things like, "How can you be gay and Christian?" It is also true that we do this to ourselves.

The boy fidgeted as boys sometimes do when forced to sit and wait when they'd rather be outside playing. He was afraid to tell the therapist the cause of the anxiety his parents had recently noticed in him. The counselor felt frustrated. The boy seemed healthy and normal, yet worn from worry.

25

The boy thought of the pleasurable experiences responsible for his concern. He had discovered that rubbing his penis offered him wonderful sensations. He didn't know why, but he automatically felt guilty about these feelings. Then, one night, in the midst of enjoying this pleasure, he was overwhelmed by what felt like blood pulsing from his body. Horrified, believing God was punishing him, he turned on the light, but found no blood. Relieved, he thought maybe it was a warning.

The following Sunday his church school teacher read a passage from Matthew which terrified him. Maybe this is where he should begin with the counselor, the boy thought. "You know, there's this verse in the Bible," the boy began fearfully, "about cutting off your hand if it makes you sin, or if any part of your body does that, you should cut it off rather than go to hell . . ."

The woman stared into her coffee for a long time after her parents left. It had been difficult enough deciding to end her five-year marriage, without her parents laying into her about the sin she was committing. Marriage had felt so imprisoning, like the time she had rheumatic fever as a child and was forced to stay home from school for a year. And she had loved school.

Her husband had seemed threatened by her every attempt to get out of the house, to grow, to learn, to develop skills, to earn money. Though she still loved him, she announced her plan to divorce. He labeled her decision "selfish." And her parents quoted Jesus: "But I say to you that every one who divorces his wife, except on the ground of unchastity, makes her an adulteress; and whoever marries her commits adultery" (Matt. 5:32).

The woman stared into her coffee, which, like her future, seemed muddy. She felt like it was a choice between her Christian faith and her life.

"You should fight it," Pete told Ann as she emptied her desk.

"No," Ann replied forcefully, trying to convince herself as well as Pete, "it wouldn't be good for the church."

"How do you know?" Pete asked, "it could be an education for the church. And think what it would mean for other gay people in this town! If people knew someone that they have always admired is a lesbian, then their minds might be changed. You owe it to yourself and to us to see this thing through."

"Look, Pete, I've spent ten years of my life building this congregation. I'm not going to be divisive now. I feel blessed that three of those ten years I had Beth as part of my life. It was our mistake to share our relationship with Jeff and Marie. We thought they'd be supportive, that we could trust them," Ann sighed.

"Yeah, and now they blackmail you into leaving. They're evil! You should fight," urged Pete.

Ann smiled at Pete's concern, but responded, "And what was it Jesus said about not resisting one who is evil, but if someone strikes you, turning the other cheek?"

Inadequately understood scriptures force many Christians into false choices: for the boy, a seeming choice between sexual pleasure and eternal life; for the married woman, an apparent choice between abundant life and Christian faith; for the pastor, a choice between pursuing her calling and keeping peace.

These vignettes are based on actual experiences, and they represent many more. The boy worries over the scriptural text most commonly quoted by children to therapists. Marriages filled with animosity and stunted personal growth are preserved every day because Jesus spoke against divorce. And members of oppressed groups have been kept in their place for the sake of peace at all costs.

Does Jesus really intend all this? Doesn't it run counter to God's charge in the Old Testament to choose life, and God's call in the New Testament for abundant life? When we feel guilty about our bodies, inhibit personal growth, or fail to stand up for our rights, aren't we choosing the opposite of abundant life?

These three situations cry out for another interpretation of the scriptures. God's truth is not nakedly presented in scripture. God's truth is cloaked in words, images, and symbols, as well as in ancient terminologies, world-views, and doctrines. Different understandings of God's truth have emerged in succeeding generations. And just as Jesus of Nazareth knew different audiences needed to hear different truths, the Jesus who continues down through history knows people of different times need to hear different truths. Scriptural interpretation must be adjudicated by the spiritual community, inspired by the Spirit and informed by biblical and other scholarship.

When Jesus spoke about sacrificing parts of the body which cause one to sin, he was not advocating self-mutilation, whether of body or desire. Rather, he was suggesting the total commitment required to cling close to God, an attitude toward God that determines behavior.

When Jesus spoke against divorce, it was to protect women of his day, who were being cut off from financial security by men wantonly divorcing them. Jesus was responding more to the mistreatment of women than of marriage.

And when Jesus advocated turning the other cheek, he was responding to the question of revenge. The old law to which he refers, "An eye for an eye and a tooth for a tooth," was meant to restrain the revenge of the injured party, so that no more violence was returned than had been received. Jesus wants his followers to go further, by transforming any need for vengeance into forgiveness, a forgiveness which rejects returning violence for violence. But this doesn't mean cooperating with injustice.

Scriptures understood to be about homosexuality have similarly been misinterpreted. Parents of a young gay man with AIDS phoned me at the church seeking pastoral care for him and them. They were from a small town in the Midwest. The son had been living in the Los Angeles area for several years. When he came home to visit them, they accidentally learned of his AIDS diagnosis and that he was gay, secrets he had kept from them for fear of their reaction.

Responding compassionately, the parents wanted to go to their pastor for support. But he had preached against homosexuality on several occasions, and they did not want to expose either themselves or their severely closeted son to his negativity. They also felt uncomfortable telling any other church member because they were afraid their concerns would be spread throughout the town. The parents were angry that, during the crisis of their lives, the church they had supported so actively was of no use to them. Through a secular AIDS network set up by the gay community, they were put in touch with another pastor from their denomination, one sympathetic and helpful.

Both the son and the parents wanted the son to be treated and, if it came to that, to die at home. But, again, the size of their town made it impossible. There was a lack of adequate medical facilities for treatment. Perhaps even more of a problem were relatives who lived nearby who were fundamentalist Christians vocally opposed to homosexuality. The son wanted privacy. So the parents returned with the son to California for his treatment. The sympathetic pastor, aware of my ministry, referred them to me.

What was remarkable to me was how welcoming the parents were to information on homosexuality and support groups, both for their son and themselves. They met with Adele and Larry Starr, founders of Parents and Friends of Lesbians and Gays. They made connections with AIDS Project/Los Angeles. And, of course, they reached out to the church through the Lazarus Project. They became strong advocates for gay people in a very short time. The mother commiserated with me when a judicial court of our Presbyterian Church rendered judgment against churches which were ordaining gay leadership. "How can they call themselves Christian and do this," she wondered, "in the midst of all the discrimination you face—and now the AIDS crisis?"

What was most grievous for me was the difficulty convincing the son that God loved him, and that AIDS was not God's punishment for either his homosexuality or his sexual activity. The parents, because they loved their son, readily believed that God loved him and would not cause this suffering. But, because the son did not love himself, he could not believe God loved him. The church and the society had done their homophobic dirty work successfully: they had taught him that he was bad because of his homosexuality and deserved God's wrath. He had not been helped to integrate his faith and his sexuality before this; now it seemed almost too late. When he died, I doubt he believed he was going home to God. My faith tells me that he had a wonderful surprise awaiting him. I'm just sad the reunion could not have been effected on this side of the threshold known as death.

A tragic episode such as this is the result of a misunderstanding of scriptures purported to be about homosexuality. This story cries out for another interpretation of those scriptures so that it might have a happier resolution, one more divinely inspired.

Many lesbians and gays suffer a tragic disability to accept God's welcome because of inadequate understanding of these scriptures. It is not only their disability, it is the disability of the church and the broader society influenced by biblical values. For I believe that an inability to accept God's welcome of others reflects an inability to accept God's welcome, period. The elder brother was clearly welcomed to the family feast, but because it celebrated the welcomed return of his prodigal brother, he declined to accept.

The Bible's primary intent is to reveal spiritual truth. Specific applications or particular expressions of spiritual truths may or may not be transferable to another setting. And not every expression of spiritual truth is detailed in the Bible. Much of this book will be applying spiritual truths from the Bible to new situations.

In bringing spiritual truths to new situations, we must be governed by the Bible's broadest themes. Choosing life, liberation from oppression, salvation from sin, God's redemption in Jesus Christ, loving God and neighbor, the community of faith—all these are important concepts for understanding how God welcomes us home and how we return home to our spirituality. For Christians, the central spiritual truth revealed in scripture is Jesus Christ, God made flesh in a sacrificially merciful lover of humankind. Within this broader context, what does or doesn't the Bible say about homosexuality?

The Bible never speaks of homosexual love nor of homosexual orientation. That a minority of persons are created homosexual and may find spiritually fulfilling love relationships with the same gender was unknown to the biblical writers. What they critiqued was behavior that gays and lesbians themselves have been critical of: homosexual rape, a gross form of inhospitality (Sodom and Gomorrah [Gen. 18–19]), men acting like women (Lev. 18:22 and 20:13), heterosexuals behaving homosexually (Rom. 1), and male prostitution (Paul's list in 1 Cor. 6). The biblical writers may have personally condemned any homosexual conduct, but their inspired writings did not do so. The writers were limited by their social context and lack of experience; the Holy Spirit is not so limited. If the Holy Spirit did not speak against homosexual love nor homosexual orientation throughout scripture, perhaps she had witnessed between homosexuals the same love she celebrated between heterosexuals.

Biblical scholars do not even consider homosexuality a *minor* theme in scripture. The few seeming references to it, listed above, are blown out of proportion. Yet often our opponents make us defensive with these lesser scriptures. Compare teachings against divorce, including one on the lips of Jesus, which have not rigidly been adhered to. Compare the many admonitions against usury, lending money at interest, opposed by the church for centuries, which we have conveniently set aside. Or think of Jesus' many calls to give up wealth for the sake of God's commonwealth, and the perversion of this by many churches which believe that personal, material wealth is a sign of God's blessing!

Once when I was on a television talk show with a fundamentalist preacher, I heard him say, "Homosexuals want to reinterpret the Bible to suit themselves. What's at stake here is the authority of scripture." I pointed out that *everyone* reinterprets the Bible to suit themselves. American Christians, for example, enjoy an average wealth that Jesus would have found appalling in the face of the poor in our local communities and our world community! But the broader implication of his statement is that there is *one* authoritative interpretation of the Bible, that any others are "*re*-interpretations" which somehow do not recognize the authority of scripture. He was blind to the beam in his own eye—he did not see that fundamentalism itself is a reinterpretation of scripture. The Reformation centuries earlier, which helped spawn fundamentalism, was also a reinterpretation of scripture. Reinterpreting scripture is indeed quite traditional!

Finally, he did not understand that nongay biblical scholars have also interpreted the biblical passages about homosexuality differently: professors like Robin Scroggs of New York's Union Theological Seminary and George Edwards of Louisville Presbyterian Theological Seminary have written books on the subject. They are two among many nongay theologians who have nothing to gain and much to lose in presenting another biblical interpretation.

"If your right hand causes you to sin, cut it off and throw it away . . ." Because of misunderstood scripture, lesbian women and gay men have been physically mutilated during certain periods of history "in the name of Christ" by those who claimed they wished to save our souls. While today's mores make this unfashionable in most countries, emotional mutilation is commonplace, whether at the hands of those who would simply deny us expression of heartfelt tenderness, or at the hands of those who go so far as to claim our very existence opposes societal ideals.

"But I say to you that every one who divorces . . ." Realistic Christians have accepted that divorces happen regardless of Jesus' admonition against it. As Jesus would, they minister compassionately to the separated partners. But if one is homosexual, she or he often does not receive ongoing support. The person is considered selfish, and homosexuality is condemned as antifamily. Ironically, though heterosexuals receive the support of the church in breaking their commitment, homosexuals receive no support and considerable abuse for *making* their commitments.

"If someone strikes you, turn the other cheek . . ." Admonished to turn the other cheek when our privacy and our rights have been trampled on, lesbian and gay Christians have been shushed so that we won't stir up trouble in the church. Closeted supporters (both gay and nongay) have chimed, "Why make a big deal of it?" Meanwhile our self-declared enemies are free to create as much trouble about homosexuality as they can. I can count on reading more about lesbian and gay Christians, albeit unfavorably biased, in reactionary church publications than in moderate and liberal ones. Gays and lesbians are frequently sacrificed to appease the false gods of the church's conservative agenda, the church's liberal agenda, or the church's economic agenda. Often we are sacrificed on the altar of a new trinity: the peace, unity, and purity of the church. I do not believe that this is what Jesus had in mind. Rather, I believe that Jesus intends that lesbian and gay Christians not respond to our opposition as they do to us. When they impugn our Christianity, we should not impugn theirs. When they try to oust us from the church, we should not try to oust them.

If only for those lesbian women and gay men of future generations, we must no longer tolerate those who seek to mutilate us, prevent our abundant life, and keep us quiet. They must be corrected. If they cannot be, we must use legislative and judicial means to restrain them from causing further mutilation, imprisonment, and death. This is needed in society and needed in the church. Called by Christ to forgive, we cannot damn them in our hearts nor return their violence. They are equally loved by God, and also need to hear God's liberating Word of love through us.

This is not just our cause; it must be the cause of the whole Body of Christ, the church. Inadequately understood scripture has mutilated the church, cutting off members; retarded the church's growth, failing to be inclusive of new people and new experience; and preserved a false sense of peace, rejecting prophetic voices. To be faithful to the Word of God in scripture requires a profound faithfulness to hearing God's welcome pronounced in the yes that is Christ.

PART II

Receiving Our Inheritance

Paul's prayer for the Ephesians coincides with my hope for this section: "that you may know what is the hope to which God has called you, what are the riches of God's glorious inheritance in the saints, and what is the immeasurable greatness of God's power in us who believe, according to the working of God's great might accomplished in Christ" (Eph. 1:18–20). The Gentiles are reminded that the community of faith is "a holy temple . . . in whom *you also* are built into it for a dwelling place of God in the Spirit" (Eph. 2:22).

Accepting Jesus Christ means much more than an assent to doctrine, it means struggling with his mystical and physical manifestations (chapter 5). Reclaiming our spirituality requires occasionally *returning to the "land of awes,"* in search of inspiration, fresh vision, and passion (chapter 6). Accepting the inheritance of our sexuality and of our gay community means *celebrating gay and lesbian pride* (chapter 7). Establishing a prayer life may become an opportunity for *developing intimacy with God* (chapter 8).

Accepting Jesus Christ

A gay man who attended a gay Alcoholics Anonymous group which met in our church was invited to worship. He would later tell me that he felt such hostility toward the church because of its mistreatment of gay people that he could not say the words "Jesus Christ." Through worship and Bible study, he soon was not only able to say the name, but to confess Jesus Christ as Lord. Several months after he joined the church, he took me aside during coffee hour following worship and said, "Chris, I have to tell you something that I think only you would understand." Hearing the urgency in his voice, I immediately led him to the church office and asked what was on his mind. "I don't think I could ever tell this to anybody else," he began. I braced myself for a serious confession. "Yesterday morning I woke up with the most profound sense of God's love. God loved me. I felt surrounded by God's love." I shared his joy in this intimate moment. In a society which eschews spiritual values, spirituality is perhaps the final frontier of intimacy. How I wish the coffee hour after church were used as an opportunity to discuss spiritual experiences like this as much as it is used for church business and gossip!

This man continued to struggle to learn more of Jesus Christ through reading, prayer, and asking questions. His distaste for the apostle Paul led him to borrow books about him, until he better understood him. He was interested in what Christians of earlier ages believed, demonstrated in his faithful attendance at Bible study and his reading of books from my library. He developed a passion for the church of the present as well. He was elected an elder, served as treasurer, and later came on staff as custodian. He helped begin a free lunch program for local street people. And he eventually led our ministry to the gay inmates of the county jail, preaching about the very one whose name he could not pronounce when first worshiping with us: Jesus Christ!

Whenever we welcomed gay or nongay members into the church, the central affirmation they were expected to make was "Jesus Christ is my Lord and Savior." Occasionally someone in the class for new members would ask for a little clarification on what the statement meant. Someone else might be surprised at that question, declaring, "Why, it's pretty straightforward." But is it? If we consider it simple, maybe we haven't really struggled with its meaning.

One person might want to know, for example, if making this affirmation devalued other religions. Another might be curious about the "job descriptions" for titles like "Lord" and "Savior." Still another might ask, "Who is Jesus Christ really, and what does it mean to accept Jesus Christ?"

Communication in the twentieth century has brought various world religions into conversation as never before. Similarities and uniquenesses have been noted by persons of faith who are not threatened by this conversation. Rapport is building among former enemies. In this country, the formation of the National Conference of Christians and Jews has contributed to interfaith dialogue, while the National Council of Churches has created ecumenical cooperation. Globally, the World Council of Churches promotes ecumenical relations, a cause that Pope John XXIII supported between Catholics and Protestants. Bridges have been built between religions in the East and the West and sharing of religious beliefs, customs, and practices has become commonplace. Shifts of populations from one world region to another have added to this phenomenon. Mahatma Gandhi, a Hindu, could consider himself Christian and Muslim as well. Thomas Merton, a renowned Catholic spiritual leader, died in his pursuit of connections and common sources among Christian, Hindu, and Buddhist spirituality. Mother Teresa is considered a saint in India, though but a fraction of its citizens are Christian. The interfaith experience is not only found among major religious organizations and spiritual giants. Even in the suburban neighborhood in which I grew up, an elaborate Buddhist temple now stands across the street from a modest Baptist church. Fledgling gay and lesbian religious groups have created interfaith coalitions in many of the country's municipalities. The Universal Fellowship of Metropolitan Community Churches continues to engage the National Council of Churches in dialogue on its interest in membership in that body.

Mainstream Protestants have often taken pride in our ecumenical spirit and our interfaith tolerance. At the same time we affirm that the central mediator of God's presence in our lives is Jesus Christ. That is, as we draw closer to Jesus Christ, we experience God. To affirm this does not necessarily entail denial that God may be revealed in other ways. To deny such a possibility may be a "culturecentric" or defensive attempt to limit God.

The early church employed the terms *Lord* and *Savior* to describe its experience of God in Christ. To use *Lord,* or the nonmale-oriented *Sovereign,* meant more to early Christians than simply ascribing sovereignty to Jesus Christ as ruler of their lives. Formerly *Lord* had been applied only to Yahweh, the God of Israel. In applying the name to Jesus, his followers intended to assert his divinity. Using the additional term *Savior* suggested their experience of Jesus delivering them from sin and death. For them, Jesus Christ served at once as high priest and sacrificial lamb, effecting in his crucifixion the atonement which reconciled them to God. His resurrection at God's hands revealed to them not only his vindication but his victory over death for all believers. Saved from sin, abundant life was now possible. Delivered from death, life took on an eternal perspective.

But there were two other ways in which Jesus delivered his followers. Not only were they delivered from sin by his own sacrifice, they were also delivered from the practice of animal sacrifice, the cumbersome process of being forgiven for sin by offering the life's blood of an animal on the altar of Yahweh. Secondly, they were delivered from the paralysis inherent in the legalistic practice of the Law of Moses which often interfered with fulfilling the intent of God's law. Jesus reminded his people that the law was made for humankind, not humankind for the law, when he healed the sick on the Sabbath, thereby breaking the law forbidding work on the Sabbath. Jesus viewed himself in the Sermon on the Mount not as one who broke the law but who fulfilled the law. The apostle Paul eloquently writes of the Christian's freedom in Christ from the Law's demands in his letter to the Romans. For Paul, the Christian's righteousness was derived not by knowledge and practice of the Law, but by faith in Jesus Christ.

The church through the ages has affirmed these understandings of Jesus. But different times and varied experience and circumstances have brought out additional nuances. The poor have seen Jesus as a sovereign who is their advocate, a friend more than a ruler. Jesus did say that the last shall be first, the least the greatest, and the servant the leader.

The oppressed have seen Jesus as saving them from the sin of oppression. Savior becomes liberator. Individual Christians are led to sacrifice themselves as Jesus did for the abundant life of the oppressed community. An eternal perspective offers hope in the knowledge that, as theologian Reinhold

Niehbur put it, that which is most worthwhile to do in life is not accomplished in a single lifetime.

Lesbians and gays who have served time or are serving time in the closet know what it means to be poor and oppressed. Within the closet, the poverty experienced may be love-deprivation. Outside the closet, the poverty may be vocational, societal, or financial. Within the closet, the oppression may be personal. Outside the closet, the oppression may be political. Such closets are the constructions of the legal paralysis which grips the church and society around sexuality. The church and society believe it is better to imprison the "deviates" in this way than to question the law, whether it be the supposed laws of God or nature, or the actual laws of states or nations.

Lesbian and gay Christians often experience Jesus Christ as friend more than ruler. Having been "lorded over" by others, we may see Jesus Christ as a benevolent sovereign in a world of malevolent political and ecclesiastical rulers. In our adversity, Jesus is our advocate. In our hunger for love and acceptance, Jesus is our lover. As such, he reveals God's loving presence in our lives.

Wanting deliverance from our imprisonment in closet-tombs, desiring abundant life, and needing an eternal perspective in our present suffering, Jesus Christ is also our liberator. Christ saves us from the oppression caused by homophobia and heterosexism, and delivers us from the binding limitations of sin and of death. Vulnerable as Lazarus in his tomb, we hear Jesus Christ call our neighbors to remove the stone of homophobia from the door of our tomb. As he calls us from closet-tombs, we hear him say, "Unbind Lazarus, and let him go," and the bonds of death are broken. As we draw closer to Jesus, we are freed from the death grip of the law and freed for the embrace of life that is love. In this liberation, we find ourselves nearer to God, who beckons us toward a future brighter than we imagined.

After attending his first Lazarus Bible study, a gay illustrator drew a detailed picture of Jesus embracing the resurrected Lazarus and giving him a kiss. This reflected the new, joyful life and loving tenderness he experienced in being welcomed home to his Christian faith within our inclusive congregation. The illustration was his way of affirming Jesus Christ as Lord and Savior.

Affirming Jesus Christ as Sovereign and Savior, Advocate and Liberator, clarifies the concept of "accepting Jesus Christ." But, for me, the concept needs embodiment, word must become flesh. Even when I was a Baptist, a denomination in which the phrase "accepting Jesus Christ" is more current than in the Presbyterian Church of which I am now a member, I puzzled over its meaning. Was it a sudden and profound solution to the riddle of life? My acceptance seemed to lead only to more riddles, questions, and struggles. And yet I heard people speak of the experience as the end-all and cure-all. There were people who thought that conversion was simple and urgent, sometimes treating it much like a desperately needed business transaction. Some thought of accepting Jesus Christ only as insurance against damnation. But I came to view conversion as a process for which a lifetime and perhaps eternity was needed, and as assurance of God's presence in that process. Some people believed that nothing was necessary after "accepting Jesus Christ." I couldn't comprehend how belief without action was enough, or even possible.

Jesus' triumphal entry into Jerusalem serves as metaphor for the acceptance of Christ. On the first Palm Sunday, as the crowds cheered Jesus into the holy city, their welcome did not mean they would not struggle with this Christ. They would not understand this Savior who lamented over the city, saying, "O Jerusalem, Jerusalem, killing the prophets and stoning those who are sent to you! How often I would have gathered your children together as a hen gathers her brood under her wings, and you would not!" (Matt. 23:37). They would not believe this Sovereign who wept as he drew near the welcoming multitudes, saying, "Would that even today you knew the things that make for peace!" (Luke 19:41–42).

Jerusalem was to question his authority, ask trick questions, question his belief in the resurrection of the dead, demand to know when the fulfillment of time would come, betray him, deny him, place him on trial, judge him, mock him, and crucify him. It would be hard to remember that this same city also accepted him with such a grand, palm-waving flourish.

Doesn't this sound familiar? Haven't most of us Christians accepted Jesus Christ with joy only to struggle with him, question his authority, doubt his assurances of resurrection, demand answers, betray him, deny him, judge him, mock him, and crucify him? Gays and lesbians know something of what Jesus felt. We too know what it means to be welcomed based upon inaccurate assumptions and expectations. We too know what it means to be betrayed, denied, judged, and mocked when formerly hospitable people turn hostile when they learn our true nature.

But there are redemptive moments in Jerusalem's acceptance of Jesus Christ, just as there are redemptive moments in our own acceptance. Accepting Jesus Christ means also confessing our sins with the criminal crucified on his right, saying, "Jesus, remember me when you come into your kingdom." Accepting Jesus Christ means standing with the women disciples unafraid to be with Jesus in his suffering on the cross. And, accepting Jesus Christ means acknowledging with the alien centurion, "Truly, this was the Child of God." (The Semitic idiom "child of . . ." meant having the essence of the parent. Hence, Jesus contained God's essence.)

Still, we are dealing with metaphor. What is the concrete nature of this Jesus Christ we are charged to accept, struggle and interact with, and yet affirm?

Traditionally, there are four manifestations of Jesus Christ. First, there is the historical Jesus who lived, taught, prayed, healed, pointed to God, caused political, religious, and social tumult, was crucified, died, was buried, and whose followers claimed to have seen resurrected. We can read of him in the books of the New Testament, particularly the Gospels, but realize these scriptures do not and cannot present all of who he was. We also realize no historical account is objective. Even more so with Jesus, for our biblical historians viewed the historical Jesus through eyes of faith.

Second, there is the mystical Jesus Christ, who transcends the place and time of the historical Jesus and touches us even today. Perhaps this is the greatest miracle of Jesus, that one who knew only the agrarian hillsides of Galilee, the wilderness of Judea, and the relatively small city of Jerusalem, could speak words whose truth still rings out through centuries of cultural change and increasing sophistication. The Spirit of Christ has led to new insights and movements. These "greater truths" which Jesus prophesied have continued to cast out demons of the Antichrist, those who would make the Spirit of Christ captive to an institution, dogma, or law. And Jesus has continued to mediate God's love by touching, lifting, and healing the poor, the oppressed, and the suffering.

Third, there is the Body of Christ, the Church, sometimes but not always to be identified with the church as institution. The Body of Christ does require a gathering of the *ecclesia*, the "called" community, to manifest itself. But it may be as small as "where two or three are gathered in [Christ's] name." The Church, as Christ's Body in the world, is charged to carry on the ministry of the historical Jesus, informed and led through prayer, meditation, scripture, and tradition by the mystical Christ. As Jesus mediated God's presence in word and deed, so the Church is called to mediate God's presence in word and sacrament and acts of mercy, justice, and grace. As such, it serves as priest, pastor, and prophet to the world.

When the institutional church fails to serve as the Church in this sense, the Spirit of Christ lifts up others who fulfill its high calling, who may or may not describe themselves as "Christian." For example, when the institutional church generally failed us in the initial years of the AIDS crisis, I believe that the Spirit of Christ, undaunted, called lesbian women and gay men into service to accomplish the ministry the church refused.

Fourth and finally, there is Christ the Stranger: the Christ who comes to us in the form of Saint Francis' leper, who, when we overcome our fear and embrace the leper, turns out to be Christ himself. Not only do we feed the hungry street person, comfort the person with AIDS, and welcome the alien refugee, but they in turn feed us, comfort us, and welcome us. We do not give to receive, but we receive with thanksgiving the gifts of the stranger and share our own abundance with them. In doing so we hear the words that Jesus spoke to the righteous in the vision of the Last Judgment in the gospel according to Matthew: "As much as you have ministered to the least of these, you have ministered unto me."

Accepting Jesus Christ, I believe, requires accepting all four of these manifestations. It means struggling with them, engaging them, interacting with them, and yet affirming them. To only accept one or two is not to fully accept Jesus. Some only want the historical or the mystical Jesus, and refuse to deal with his body either in the church or in the stranger. But this disembodiment is as bad as the disembodiment forced on lesbians and gays by those who insist we neglect our sexuality for the sake of a disembodied spirituality. And some Christians get caught up exclusively dealing with the church as Christ's Body or serving Christ the Stranger, ignoring the historical and mystical Jesus. This is similar to sexual expressions that are uninspired by the spirit of love and caring: not bad, but not as fulfilling. I believe that, for the Christian, all forms of Jesus Christ are to be accepted and contended with. That is what "accepting Jesus Christ" means.

The gay man whose story I told at the beginning of this chapter, who at first could not say "Jesus Christ" because of the church's mistreatment of lesbians and gays, accepted Jesus Christ in these four ways. He learned of the historical Jesus through scripture. He meditated on the mystical Jesus in prayer. He became involved with the church as the Body of Christ, both the church of the past and of the present. And he embraced Christ the Stranger in feeding the street people and preaching good news to jail inmates. All because he found a church which welcomed him home, and awakened him to God's love.

CHAPTER 6

Returning to the "Land of Awes"

Returning home to our Christian faith does not mean we will never feel restless again. A Buddhist scholar visiting Santa Barbara, California, claimed to have experienced Nirvana in his meditation exercises. "What's left after accomplishing your goal?" a student asked. The monk replied wisely, "I have also arrived in Santa Barbara, but have not yet seen everything there is to see. So it is with Nirvana." Just because one has gained a centering, an anchor, for one's life does not mean she or he will not also experience a divine restlessness.

When you moved to this gay neighborhood, you thought all your problems would be answered. Now you find yourself standing alone in the bar—again. It's Saturday night, halfway through a lonely weekend. You've distracted yourself all day with home chores. Now you must face the reality that:

a) you made no plans for tonight;
b) you got stood up tonight;
c) she or he didn't call to make plans;
d) you decided to be spontaneous;
e) none of the above;
f) all of the above.

Searching the faces in the bar for a glimmer of hope, intellect, or happiness, checking the bodies for curves, bulges, and flat stomachs, you say to yourself, disgusted with this endless search, "Is this all there is?"

Monday. How you hate to go to work on Mondays. Return to the routine, and the routine reminder that you were born for more than this—that at least you *want* more than what this job can offer. Not more money, though that would be nice; rather, more satisfaction, more fulfillment, more challenge. Or perhaps you want less: less tension, less anxiety, less busy-ness. You acknowledge the more-or-less, grass-always-greener syndrome. And you wonder, "Is this all there is?"

Tuesday night. You meet with the committee of your local AIDS organization. Everyone's complaining that not enough is being done to meet the crisis. And everyone, including yourself, seems to be burning out, overburdened by the extraordinary dimensions—political and personal—of the AIDS pandemic. You work together on a conference to involve more members of the community, and end up squabbling over the prioritizing of issues to be presented. You think to yourself, "Is this all there is?"

Thursday night. You and your lover have just finished leftover spaghetti and have settled down on the sofa for another night of TV. Sounds attractively homey to single folk who have never experienced it, but you feel vaguely discontent as you tune in a detective series with a good-looking protagonist. It's a rerun, but you watch it anyway, because you can't remember if you've seen it. A sitcom is the high point of the evening. Another series grabs your attention. You assure yourself this one is educational and cultural, since it's received such good reviews. But deep within a voice whispers, "Is this all there is?"

Sunday morning worship. An hour to be filled with thanks and praise. An hour to enjoy and celebrate God's presence in the world. An hour to be with your family of faith, a group of good friends. It is announced that, during coffee hour, one committee needs help packing lunches for the street people and another committee needs volunteers to prepare a mailing. You plan to avoid coffee hour, though you'll miss greeting friends. Then you hear a sentence pronounced against you: your committee will have a "brief" two-hour meeting directly following the worship service. There goes brunch. The congregation stands to sing a hymn, one filled with nineteenth-century theology—or eighteenth- or seventeenth-century—and you wonder why the words catch in your throat as you think, "Is this all there is?"

"O sing a new song to God, who has done marvelous things," the Psalmist wrote (Ps. 98:1). "These things I have spoken to you, that my joy may be in you, and that your joy may be full," Jesus said (John 15:11). The Psalmist wants us to sing a new song. Jesus wants our joy to be full. This may account for the divine restlessness within us which makes us eternal pilgrims in search of new songs and full joy. I believe this divine restlessness is our spirituality.

Worldly concerns try to muzzle our restlessness: earning money, gaining possessions, building empires. When the church behaves in a worldly fashion, it too begins to muzzle our spirit. At its best, though, the church seeks to harness our spirit, much as windmills harness the wind to grind grain or generate electricity. The church wants to make our divine restlessness useful in serving others. There's nothing wrong with this, except that, just as windmills do not try to catch all the wind, churches and other volunteer organizations shouldn't try to make all of our spirituality useful. The wind must play, explore, and be free to be useless at times.

Jesus said of the Spirit that it "blows where it wills." I believe it manifests itself in the divine restlessness that makes gays and lesbians question, in the bar, on the job, in a committee, in a relationship, and in church, "Is this all there is?" For, like the divine restlessness which led people of faith out of the bondage of Egypt, out of the wilderness, and out of a spiritual legalism, so too may it lead us to freedom, to promised lands, to God's spiritual commonwealth of grace.

Jesus described the commonwealth of God as a mustard seed, which, "when it has grown . . . is the greatest of shrubs and becomes a tree, so that the birds of the air come and make nests in its branches" (Matt. 13:31–32). Blowing in the breeze of our divine restlessness are the mustard seeds of our spiritual commonwealth. They seek fertile ground in which to light, to be nurtured, nourished, and sustained. I believe that the most fertile ground for them is the "land of awes," not the Oz that lies "over the rainbow," but the one available to us in the midst of our everyday experience.

When was the last time you were struck with awe? Yet that experience is the basis for the scripture, the worship, and the faith "traditioned," or handed down, to us. If we miss the experience of awe, we miss the full impact of scripture, worship, and faith. There's no reason to believe the experience of awe is less available to us than to our spiritual ancestors. There are reasons to believe these experiences are *more* available, what with the increasing opportunities for travel, communication, and leisure.

We may deny ourselves opportunities to experience awe. Friends of mine honeymooned in Yosemite. They didn't enjoy it because, everywhere they turned, they were struck with awe: the grandeur of the towering cliffs, pounding waterfalls, tall forests, and deep valleys. Michelle admitted, "We like nature in small doses: a nice little stream, a small grove of trees . . ." "Yes," Gary added, "everywhere we turned, we'd gasp 'Ahh!'"

Too often our desires parallel those of Gary and Michelle. We want our experience of the world in tidy little packages—safe, easy-to-swallow capsules which will not overwhelm us nor overpower us. Wanting to remain "in control," we keep an arm's length from those who seem to have lost control: charismatics, enthusiasts, zealots, fanatics. Jaded to the wonders of life, we may say things like, "Nothing surprises me anymore." A hotel chain picked up on our mood to avoid surprise when it advertised, "The best surprise is no surprise." This unintended Orwellian doublespeak clouds the reality that no surprise is, after all, no surprise. Sometimes, cynical of religious or political passion, we may respond, "I don't know what to believe anymore."

Many of us don't care to be overwhelmed by the feelings within us, either. Some of us don't want to care too much, to be overtaken with grief, anger, fear, or love. We punish erotic feelings with verbal cold showers or suppressing silence. The wonder of cuddling, caressing, and orgasm is reduced to "getting off," its amnesic bliss and sweet sensation perceived as beastly rather than godly, base rather spiritual, an occasion for guilt rather than gratitude.

There's a part of us that wants to get on with the business of life, business as usual: survival, ambition, facing political "realities" rather than spiritual mysteries. There's nothing wrong with addressing the business of life. To get bogged down in spiritual mystery may become self-indulgent. But to avoid it altogether is self-abuse. For it is the mystery, the surprise, the overwhelming awe which sparks passion, fascination, imagination, and spirit to inspire the business of life as well as the worship of God.

Even scientists who follow the predictable laws of physics truly wonder at the quantum theory, which suggests that there are "jumps" in energy levels at the molecular level, when physicists would have supposed gradual increases or decreases. (From this we gain the descriptive phrase "quantum leap," which is employed to suggest an abrupt advance in knowledge or information.) This has led Process theologians to conclude that a theology without novelty or spontaneity cannot adequately account for reality.

One morning, I faced a choice. I could read the newspaper, filled with reminiscences of the horrors of World War II and the lessons supposedly learned from Vietnam. I could continue editing videotapes from a consultation on homophobia. Or I could read the cover story of *Time* magazine, which asked, "Did Comets Kill the Dinosaurs?" The first choice was politically responsible, the second choice fit my Protestant work ethic, but the third seemed an unnecessary diversion. I chose the unnecessary diversion. Feeling burdened by political realities, ready to scream if I heard the term "homophobia" one more time, I thirsted for inspiration.

I was struck with awe as I read of 26-million-year life cycles here on earth, as I discovered how little and how much we know of the universe, and as I realized how small is human history and yet how amazing is human ability to perceive the wonders of creation. To paraphrase the Psalmist, I wondered, "Who are we that God is mindful of us? And yet God has made us a little less than angels" (Ps. 8:4).

Once upon a time, when I opened a newspaper, I read the articles on religion first; now I go directly to the science articles. Too often religion seems caught up in irrelevant traditions and petty concerns. It's difficult for me to believe that some Christian traditions still do not ordain women, and that many Christians still quibble over seemingly trivial differences in rituals. Science articles give me something religion used to offer: a greater sense of the awesomeness of God.

Essentially, what the article about dinosaurs and what other science articles offer me is the mystery of God. They serve as mini-retreat experiences, momentary opportunities to gain perspective on everyday life. If the church could return to the "land of awes," I believe that the greatest gift that it could offer to future generations of human civilization is an opportunity to visit church retreat and conference centers to reflect on life: its possibilities, its dreams, its purpose and meaning. Lazarus Project conducted two retreats per year, and each was an opportunity for awe as we enjoyed the beauty of nature, one another, and of God. God was present to us not only in nature and in each other, but also in the words of scripture and tradition and in the silences of prayer and meditation. We prayed for our local congregation, the church at large, our community, and the world, as much as we prayed for ourselves. We photographed our experience, but the pictures served as pale reflections of the awe we experienced. Anyone who has tried to capture a sunset on film knows something is lost in translation. "You had to be there!" we say.

This, too, is the limitation of scripture. Scriptures are but pale reflections of the awe our spiritual ancestors enjoyed. "You had to be there!" they would say. We have to be there! We have to take the unnecessary diversion to experience awe. Otherwise we can never fully understand the awe of those who have passed their faith on to us. Otherwise we can never fully celebrate our faith in worship. Otherwise the business of life remains uninspired, and we ask, "Is this all there is?"

"O sing a new song to God, who has done marvelous things." "These things I have spoken to you, that my joy may be in you, and that your joy may be full." What can lead us to new songs, that our joy may be full? What can return us to the "land of awes?" I offer a few possibilities.

The first comes under the rubric, "and a little child shall lead them." The majority of gay men and lesbian women may not have regular access to the wonder of babies, of children discovering the world, of adolescents dreaming and loving. Yet these have much to teach all of us about life's glory as they experience it for the first time. Those of us who are parents have a wonder-full opportunity for renewal in seeing the world through the eyes of their children.

Those of us who are not parents may still enjoy this opportunity through nieces and nephews, or volunteering as a Big Brother or Big Sister or as a teacher's aide at local schools or childcare facilities. Of course, many of us choose vocations which bring us into regular contact with children, such as teaching, Christian education, or youth work. And we may also choose to be parents, through artificial insemination, adoption, or foster care.

Sometimes, we in the gay community have judgmentally viewed friendships between older men and younger men, and between older women and younger women. But, while these older-younger friendships may or may not have erotic components, a prime motivating factor for the older person is the simple joy of seeing the world anew through the fresh eyes and energy of youth. And the young person appreciates the experienced and more secure view of the older one. The popular gay entertainers Romanovsky and Phillips sing of this phenomenon in a song with the delightful refrain, "Were you robbing the cradle, or was I robbing the rocking chair?" Interestingly, a ten-year age difference between lovers in our community is not uncommon and may prove helpful to the stability of both relationship and partners.

Others of us have met our need for childlike wonder and play by caring for pets or cultivating plants. When in college, I lived in a home with a retriever who occasionally dropped a ball in my lap while I studied, reminding me to take time to play. Animals give adults permission to play and to act silly as we play games with them, talk to them, tickle and rub them. Plants invite us to relax and enjoy the beauty of nature renewing itself in yearly cycles. A close gay friend wrote me recently that what I described as my prayer life, he seemed to accomplish working in his rooftop garden.

Periodically I read children's books by which I am led as a child to understandings often more profound and moving than those found in works of theology and philosophy. Among my favorites: *Charlotte's Web*, *The Velveteen Rabbit*, *Whobody There?*, *The Little Prince*, *The Narnia Chronicles*, *The Wizard of Oz*, and Oscar Wilde's fairy tales, especially *The Happy Prince*. Reading these aloud to a lover or friend creates a healing, comforting atmosphere.

Not unlike letting a child lead us, a second possibility for returning to the "land of awes" is letting an artist lead us. In Kazantzakis' *Zorba the Greek*, Zorba and the narrator spoke seriously and practically about the business of their mine, when suddenly Zorba kicked a stone, causing it to roll downhill. Stopping in amazement, as if he were seeing such a thing for the first time, he observed: "On slopes, stones come to life again." Kazantzakis felt deep joy as he recognized this was how visionaries and poets view the world: as a child, as if for the first time. This is the gift of the artist. Art that is visual, written, or performed (in concert or on stage) may offer us a fresh sense of the world as well as new hope for human possibility. I believe, for example, that films have the possibility of becoming the sermons of the twentieth century, recovering the sense of awe and myth often lost in our attempts to demythologize religion or make it practical. They also may bring us closer to the lives of saints, religious and political, which inspire our own causes.

Sadly, many of us would not necessarily include scripture and church tradition as a way to return to the "land of awes." I list it third, not because of lesser importance, but because it incorporates both the wonder of a child and the skill and maturity of the artist. If we could read scriptures as children, yet with appreciation of its spiritual artistry and understanding of its classic truths, we would come closer to the awe of ancient people of faith. By reading scriptures as children I mean taking it at faith value, not necessarily face value. By appreciation of its spiritual artistry I mean avoiding literalism and embracing the symbolic. By understanding its classic truths, I mean discerning what is really vital to our living today. This is heresy to many, but, in effect, *all scripture was not created equal!* For Christians, the central Word in scripture is Jesus Christ as God's Word of love to us. All other words are up for discussion.

Meditating on familiar scriptures and discovering unfamiliar ones may spark imagination and faith. Yet the Bible is not the only source of inspired words. Christians who have gone before us, who have struggled with many of the same questions we do, have much to offer us. Surprisingly, many of these respected figures dealt with the relationship of sensuality/sexuality and spirituality. Saint Julian of Norwich, Saint Teresa of Avila, and Saint Anselm are but a few of those who directly and affirmingly applied sensual and sexual imagery to their devotion to God and to others. John Boswell's *Christianity, Social Tolerance, and Homosexuality* has done milestone work uncovering centuries of the Christian tradition's relationship with homosexuality.

Inspired writing is not something in the past. Contemporary words may be more vital, words such as those of Henri Nouwen, James B. Nelson, Mary Daly, Rosemary Radford Reuther, Christin Lore Weber, Thomas Merton, Simone Weil, Etty Hillesum, Robert McAffee Brown, Matthew Fox, Dorothy Donnelly, and Gustavo Gutiérrez. Inspired words written out of our own gay and lesbian Christian experience are even more relevant—for example, the writings of Malcolm Boyd, Virginia Ramey Mollenkott, John Fortunato,

Carter Heyward, Brian McNaught, and John McNeill. In my own prayer life, devotionals written by J. Barrie Shepherd, Louis Evely, Michel Quoist, Hans Ruedi-Weber, and others have been helpful in teaching me how to pray and in sharing prayer with others.

Children, artists, or spiritual teachers may lead us in returning to the "land of awes" because they bring us into new relationships with everything we experience. New relationships may be the fourth way to return to a sense of awe. Remember how excited you've become upon meeting a new friend or a potential new lover, or discovering within yourself a fresh interest or unknown talent, or developing new methods of accomplishing familiar tasks, or joining a support group or social group?

Taking trips to places we've never been, or visiting sites we've rarely seen, we literally see things as if for the first time. We may be brought into new relationship with our earth environment. Changing our usual routines—getting up early to read, run, or pray; skipping lunch to take a walk or write poetry; walking along the shore or in the park after work at sunset; reshuffling our agenda during work hours; taking time to play during our off hours—all of these create new relationships with time. New relationships revitalize us, whether the relationships are with individuals, activities, groups, environments, or time.

When we lose the "awe" experience of people, we often move on to new friends, lovers, communities, even cities. But instead of breaking faith or covenant with those who have awed us before, wouldn't it be better to find new ways of relating? I was a member of a support group that was losing the interest of its participants. Initiating a radically different format fostered a renewed interest in one another. A gay friend, tired of the bar scene, encouraged his friends to meet him for dinner, or bowling, or a movie, and bring their gay friends so everyone could meet one another in a different setting. Couples attend marriage encounter weekends or go into therapy to rediscover their previous fascination with one another. My personal therapy led me to a new relationship with myself, discovering a sense of awe at my own capability and possibilities. Renewed relationships, even with ourselves, may also renew our sense of wonder.

A little child, an artist, stories of faith, fresh or refreshed relationships may lead us to awe. As they do, they create in us a sense of worth—a valuing of our life experience and of ourselves. The English word *worship* comes from root words meaning "to shape" or "to create worth." To me this implies that the act of worship is one in which worth is created. Viewing life through the wonder of a child, the achievement of an artist, the eyes of faith, and the embodiment of relationships, creates worth. Each way of viewing life, each renewal of awe, becomes an act of worship. And worship in turn may include play and wonder (mystery), creative approaches and aesthetic expression (beauty), persons and stories of faith (spirituality), and relationships with God and one another (community). Worship, then, may become a fifth way to return to the "land of awes."

Many people treat worship like a filling station, where they will get their inspiration for the week. But worship which leads to a sense of self-worth cannot be achieved in one hour per week on Sunday mornings. Worship, the creation of worth, requires every hour of the week. This is especially important for lesbian and gay Christians, who frequently have their worth questioned during the Sunday morning hour. Worship more likely happens for us in our play, our creativity, our prayer life, and our own community. If it takes place in a church, too, we are all the more blessed.

The "land of awes" to which we return is the fertile ground which will nourish the mustard seed of faith into the fully grown commonwealth of God, God's common spiritual wealth for all creation. As we witness its growth, it will be easier to respond enthusiastically to the Psalmist's exhortation: "O sing a new song to God, who has done marvelous things." And we will understand Jesus saying to us: "These things I have spoken to you, that my joy may be in you, and that your joy may be full."

CHAPTER 7

Celebrating Gay and Lesbian Pride

The recovery of a sense of awe at our life experience creates a valuing of it. Valuing our personal experience contributes to our belief in self-worth. A healthy pride results. The current political and spiritual movement of gay and lesbian pride expresses our recovery of a sense of awe at our experience and a valuing of it. I say "current," because there have been other gay and lesbian pride movements throughout history, most recently in Germany prior to the Nazi rise to power. That the movement was destroyed and a quarter of a million of us were murdered in concentration camps serves as a sobering reminder of the ebb and flow of our acceptance. Some who participated in those murders were themselves homosexuals who did not enjoy a sense of self-worth—all the more reason for us to share our sense of pride with others.

A gay member of our congregation once told me that he never participated in gay pride parades because "a bunch of half-naked men dancing on the back of a Mack truck is not my idea of gay pride." Celebration of who we are is fun, but sometimes, in our exuberance, we might indulge in the pride which isolates and alienates us from one another and from both church and society. The Greeks used the term *hubris* to connote human arrogance in the face of the gods. It is the downfall of many an otherwise noble character in Greek tragedies. This false pride was considered by early Christians as one of the seven deadly sins. It is the mistaken notion that we are complete in and of ourselves, that we may disregard God, gay brothers, lesbian sisters, other people, other countries, the rest of creation.

But, truthfully, I felt put off by the parishioner's comment about gay pride parades. There was a harsh, judgmental tone to his voice that made me feel that he might benefit from examining his own pride. It made me think of David's wife Michal berating him for dancing half-naked in the streets of Jerusalem. The half-naked men on the Mack truck are biblically in good company. The greatest hero of the Old Testament, King David, also danced in a parade clothed only in a linen *ephod,* a small ceremonial apron. He was taking pride and joy in bringing the Ark of the Covenant (which contained the Law of Moses) into his capital city, solidifying his reign and centralizing his kingdom's power. No doubt personal pride fired his spirit alongside patriotic and religious passion.

What does gay pride mean for lesbian and gay Christians? Is it the flexing of our muscle when the patrons of New York's gay Stonewall Inn fought back the police raid in 1969? It was the first time we rebelled together as one community against the harassment common at the time, and many historians mark the beginning of the present gay political movement from that date. Or is it the proclamation of the gospel to a gay man in a bar who cried, "Nobody loves me!" and the Rev. Troy Perry responded, "Jesus loves you." This led Perry to gather twelve people for worship in 1968, the year prior to Stonewall. Thus began the Universal Fellowship of Metropolitan Community Churches (UFMCC), the world's largest lesbian and gay association. Or does our gay pride originate in the ordination of the Rev. William Johnson in 1972 by the United Church of Christ, a first and rare ordination of an openly gay person by a mainstream

62   RECEIVING OUR INHERITANCE

denomination? Both the formation of UFMCC and Johnson's ordination led to the development of lesbian/gay caucuses and support groups in every Christian tradition and denomination.

I believe that all of these stirred our sense of pride in the gay community. But they served as midwives of a pride already in our womb. A new advent was upon us. For our pride had already been conceived in our adversity.

It was the Hebrews' pride which, despite their oppression, enabled them to confront Pharaoh. Their belief that God valued them had not dissipated in the face of a harsh enslavement—indeed, it made them aware that God called them out of bondage.

It was Esther's pride in her people which caused her to confront King Ahasuerus on their behalf, despite the risk that "coming out of the closet" as a Jew would bring. Despite her rapid advancement within the king's court, she shared in the suffering of her people.

It was Mary's pride in her calling which enabled her to endure the shame of an unwed pregnancy and bear the burden of her child's later suffering, so that, as she rejoices, "all generations will call me blessed, for God who is mighty has done great things for me . . . God has put down the mighty from their thrones, and exalted those of low degree" (Luke 1:48, 49, 52).

It was the apostle Paul's pride in God's strength manifest in his weakness which led him to confront Gentiles with the gospel and confront the church with his ministry of taking the gospel to the Gentiles. "If I must boast, I must boast of the things that show my weakness," he wrote the Corinthians, "for when I am weak, I am strong" (2 Cor. 11:30, 12:10).

Outsiders mistakenly believe that gay communities or gay churches and temples are formed around sexual orientation. Rather, I believe that our communities and congregations are formed around our shared experience of adversity, suffering, and vulnerability in the face of pervasive homophobia and heterosexism. Our communities and churches and temples also celebrate our responses to our experience: our political achievements of liberation, our personal risks of identification with our people (even from within the closet), our vocational commitments to better our community, and our spiritual accomplishments of humble, compassionate service. Outsiders mistakenly believe that our pride focuses in our sexual orientation, when in reality we accept our orientation as a gift and take pride in it as anyone might who is given something that is good. We rather take pride in our accomplishments together, despite the tremendous odds against us. That is the greater source of lesbian and gay pride.

But our pride is not without tears. A few years ago, tears of pride came to my eyes when I drove past the Hollywood Bowl's electronic marquee as it flashed out its message in lights: "Christopher Street West Presents"—and then, with large letters moving across the bottom—A GAY NIGHT AT THE BOWL.

I was returning home from visiting a friend just diagnosed with AIDS who was nonetheless determined to live. We had met for lunch in a shopping center in my suburban hometown of North Hollywood. It seemed strange to be transparently gay in the town where I had grown up. Now, as I returned to my current home of West Hollywood, where it seems strange *not* to be gay, I felt deep joy that, despite all we've been through, we who are lesbian or gay still celebrate who we are and who we are becoming. We've come so far, and yet have so far to go.

Later that week, as the Bowl filled with lesbians and gays to hear the musical talents of gay choruses and bands from Dallas, Houston, Los Angeles, Minneapolis, New York, Phoenix, San Francisco, and Washington, D.C., we took pride in our numbers and in our diversity. As the combined bands movingly rendered two patriotic songs, "America the Beautiful" and "The Battle Hymn of the Republic," tears of pride filled my eyes once more as the best of American values came to mind. Our country has come so far, and yet has so far to go.

Gay and Lesbian Pride Sunday arrived. A member of our church gave a last-minute pep talk to those who would carry the "West Hollywood Presbyterian Church" banner in front of our contingent as we marched in the Los Angeles version of the nationwide celebration, the Christopher Street West Parade (named for the street in Greenwich Village where the Stonewall Inn was located). Surrounded by thirty-five colorfully clad, balloon-festooned marchers from our congregation, Rev. Peg Beissert and I rode on the back of a convertible through the parade. Peg, sixty-something, could not have been more supportive of us all if she were lesbian! As we waved to the crowds, they waved back and cheered. Peg turned to me and laughed, "One could get a big head from this!"

Toward the end of the parade, we came upon the usual group of fundamentalist Christians who come every year to the parade to wave their Bibles as weapons and swear damnation at us. As we approached, our church contingent infuriated these possessed souls even more. But, overwhelming the bullhorns of these religious gay-bashers, the lesbian women and gay men opposite them on the parade route welcomed us with the loudest cheers and applause we had received. The image I remember is of sullen and angry Christians on the left, drably dressed in black and white, but smiling and happy gays and lesbians on the right, colorfully dressed. Pharisees to the left, children of God's commonwealth on the right. Thank God we were there as a congregation to give balance to this mob on the left claiming to represent God and the church. Tears of pride came to my eyes. The church has come so far, and yet has so far to go.

What are tears of pride? A therapist will quickly tell you that tears always indicate pain or grief. In the midst of my pride, what was the pain and the grief?

We've come so far as a lesbian and gay community, and yet have so far to go. Proclaiming a "gay night" at the Hollywood Bowl, we still feel self-conscious being gay in the suburbs, and more so in remote places. Despite advancing out of closets of death and isolation, we struggle with AIDS and AIDS anxiety, which kills us or keeps us from intimate embrace. That's the pain and grief that causes tears to accompany pride.

Our country has come so far, and yet has so far to go. So many men and women—including gays and lesbians—have lived and died to defend all we believe in as Americans. But we've not fully lived up to the ideals of our Declaration of Independence, our Constitution and its Bill of Rights. We fail to recognize *all* are created equal, with inalienable rights, worthy of equal protection under the law. We have not been all that we can be as a nation. That's the pain and grief that causes tears to accompany pride.

Our church has come so far, and yet has so far to go. There are congregations which welcome gay people, but the vast majority of churches do not acknowledge, let alone *welcome* and begin to understand, our gay sisters and brothers. The religious right exerts political pressure on presidents and Congress, raining condemning words on our parade. The inertia of mainstream liberal churches, paralyzed by econophobia (my own word for their irrational fear of losing members and money) even more than homophobia, do more damage by their lack of involvement than do the more fanatical fundamentalists who openly attack us. That's the pain and grief that causes tears to accompany pride.

However, pride unaccompanied by tears may be a danger signal. If we, as lesbians and gays, forget the pain of those still struggling to accept themselves or to be themselves within their own communities, our pride becomes a smug self-indulgence. If we, as lesbian and gay Americans, forget the pain of those who still suffer oppression in this and other countries, and feel no grief for those who have sacrificed their lives or their livelihoods for the ideals of this nation and of our cause, our pride becomes blind patriotism and ingratitude. And if we, as lesbian and gay Christians, forget the pain of those who do not have a congregation they can call home, and feel no grief for those who still suffer under mistaken interpretations of scripture, our pride becomes self-righteous satisfaction.

Jesus once told his disciples that he sent them out as sheep in the midst of wolves. He warned them to be shrewd as serpents, but gentle as doves. He alerted them to the fact that they'd be treated harshly, by family and strangers, government officials and religious leaders. He advised them to avoid persecution, but if their leader was persecuted, they could expect the same treatment. But, he consoled them, they should not be anxious because the Spirit would tell them what to say and how to speak. "What I tell you in the dark, utter in the light; and what you hear whispered, proclaim upon the housetops. And do not fear those who kill the body but cannot kill the soul, rather fear the one who can destroy both soul and body in hell" (Matt. 10:27–28).

Gay and lesbian Christians might hear Jesus this way: "Don't be afraid, because the closets are going to be emptied, everything is going to come out: *their* hatred, *your* love, *my* love for *you*. What I whisper in your heart, the truth of my love for you, proclaim in parades and festivals. Don't be afraid of those who are out to limit your rights or kill you—they can't get to your soul. Only you can allow your soul to die by denying God's love for you. Birds are cheap, but nothing happens to one without God caring. You're worth a lot more!"

Lesbian and gay pride festivities are ways we shout from rooftops what we've heard in our hearts: that we are loved, that we are lovable, that we are capable of loving. They are more than a celebrative party; they are a serious proclamation of the gospel.

One of the debates I hear each year during gay pride week is whether the central festivity is a parade or a march. Is it a parade, like Mardi Gras, in which we enjoy ourselves and our diversity, no matter how the media might cover it? Or is it a political march in which we protest discrimination, prejudice, and bigotry? I believe it is both, for celebrating our community spirit is protesting all that which holds us down. The tears of pride we share suggest we have not forgotten what it was like before, nor what it is like still for those removed from our community by distance or closets.

One Lesbian and Gay Pride Sunday, I preached a sermon on the name of the Los Angeles event: "Christopher Street West." "Christopher" means "Christ-bearer," one who embodies Christ to others. It is not only the many Christian groups marching in the parade that do this. I believe that all those who participate are bearers of Christ's inclusive and compassionate message of justice.

"Street" may remind us of how we were forced onto the streets to find one another, rather than allowed to meet in homes, in churches, at work, or at play. Political awareness challenged us to "come out of the closet and into the streets" to protest discrimination. The early church had a similar experience. Excluded from synagogues, they preached the gospel in the streets. The New Testament was written in street language. Graffiti on the street—the fish symbol—indicated places where Christians could gather secretly. And the early church was not known as a building or institution, but as The Way. Christians were people of The Way.

Finally, *west* is merely a geographical designation, but, from ancient times, the West has been associated with the home of the gods, the life beyond, paradise, the New Eden of the New World, the future, God's kingdom. Naturally this is because the sun heads westward, giving a sense that all life is headed there too. Christopher Street West. Christopher: Christ-bearer. Street: the Way. West: the new world. Christopher Street West: Christ-bearer on the way to a new realm. I know what you may be thinking: this is a long way from the vision of the half-naked men dancing on the flatbed of a Mack truck. And it certainly is reading more into the name of the Los Angeles parade and festival than was intended. But a spiritual vision is not truth in the sense of reality. It is truth in the sense of meaning. To those with eyes to see, this could be the meaning of all lesbian and gay pride parades and marches.

When our church's parade contingent approached running the gauntlet between the booing, biblical bandits who rob the Bible of its true meaning, and the cheering and cheerful lesbian women and gay men who search and hope for true meaning from the church, the band before us played the old spiritual, "When the Saints Go Marching In." It seemed theologically appropriate, for those of us marching and those cheering us on were, in doing so, most authentically praying, "Lord, I want to be in that number, when the saints go marching in." And, as our own kazoo band struck up "Jesus Loves Me," it was amazing to me how many people in the crowd knew the words.

CHAPTER 8

Developing Intimacy with God

Knowing God loves us does not mean that we experience God's love every day. But we can, if we choose to. Brother Thomas Keating, author of *Open Mind, Open Heart*, uses the model of lovers in describing our developing relationship with God.[1] If you grow to love someone, you want to spend time with her or him, getting to know the person. Meditating upon scripture and cultivating a listening prayer become ways of getting to know God. Though done in private, this is not done in isolation. Spiritual counsel is needed from others in the Christian community, whether through worship, education, books, or spiritual advisors. But, just as lovers need time to be alone, so you and God need time to be together without distraction.

I needed to get in touch with God in a fresh way in the early years of my ministry. I'd weathered storms of controversy, first in a nationwide debate on the ordination of gays and lesbians, then leading a ministry reconciling the church and the gay community. Like the early disciples of Jesus who were caught in a storm on the Sea of Galilee, I felt a sense of panic, wondering where the boat was going, losing the vision of horizon that was our destination, wanting to shake Christ's body into action to save me, to save us.

I needed to do something dramatic, so I visited the Holy Land. In Jerusalem, hoping to find Christ's spirit, I walked the Via Dolorosa, the Way of Sorrows, the unlikely but traditional path of Jesus to his cross. But I did not find Jesus Christ there.

Just as some biblical accounts of the resurrection claimed, he went before me into Galilee. Staying in a kibbutz alongside the Sea of Galilee, I began to sense the facet of Christ's spirit I needed to feel at the time: that part which reassured my faith by calming troubled waters around me and within my soul, saying, "Peace! Be still!"

During my visit, our travel group joined two other groups on a boat trip across the water. In the middle of the lake, the boat's engine was switched off, so that we might experience the peacefulness of the water, appreciating its spiritual dimensions. But, as in the story from the fourth chapter of Mark's gospel that I earlier alluded to, a storm suddenly arose. This time it was a storm of words. For the leaders of the other two groups—fundamentalist Christians—felt compelled to get on the boat's public address system and offer lengthy prayers, disturbing the precious silence. "We just thank you, Jesus, dear, sweet Jesus, for this most beautiful day. It's just so wonderful to be here, where you rebuked the seas so long ago, and where your spirit may still be felt . . ." Thus began a fifteen-minute squall of wordy prayers.

Our group, half Jewish, found ourselves wishing Jesus were here now to rebuke this gushing flood of sentimental, parochial religion. My own negative reaction grew from once having *been* there: I was reared in a fundamentalist tradition, among people confident of our answers, so clear about God's plan for our lives and the lives of others, so cocky with our "intimate" knowledge of God's nature and will. But God had other plans for my life. I was homosexual. And though Jesus, in the miracle story of a storm at sea, took charge of natural forces and turned them around, he had not chosen to take charge of the natural sexual urges within me and turn them around. Instead, in my long conversations with God, asking why, pleading for help, panicked, it was as if Jesus spoke to me the same words he said to his anxious disciples on the Sea of Galilee: "Peace! Be still! Why are you afraid? Have you no faith?"

"Be still and know that I am God," exhorts the Psalmist (Ps. 46:10). In Mark's story of the storm at sea, two expressions of spirituality are contrasted. One is expressed by the disciples who come to Jesus in a panic, symbolic of those who rely on spirituality primarily in times of emergency. There is nothing wrong with that, except that external storms of our lives frequently engender internal storms born of our fears, demands, and expectations—of God or of others—storms that need calming. The other form of spirituality, the one that Jesus expressed, is based in the trust that grows from intimacy with God, from a regular, disciplined prayer life. This trust and this faith allowed Jesus to sleep through a turbulent storm, yet, when urged, to address the storm with spiritual power.

The "fear of God" we so frequently hear about from pulpits and read about in scripture was never intended to serve as a psychological description of our relationship with God, though that is how it has often been interpreted. Rather, "fear of God" suggests our theological relationship with God. A healthy respect is an appropriate response to a God whose awesome power calls life into being, and yet offers us a loving covenant relationship. The more we realize the life-giving and loving nature of God's relationship with us, the greater our trust in God becomes. Jesus' trust was great enough that the storm at sea did not even wake him. When the disciples chastised him for his seemingly detached attitude, Jesus' spirituality empowered him to rebuke the volatile forces of

faithlessness stirred up within their hearts. Spiritually, bringing peace to troubled hearts is a miracle of larger significance
than calming clouds and waves.

"Peace! Be still!" Jesus said to the winds and the sea. This
rebuke in the Greek is far more forceful than it appears in
translation, as if Jesus were casting out a demon. Perhaps it
was a demon that prevented listening for God, or listening
to others, in silence—not empty silence, or stony silence, but
an expectant silence, a listening and prayerful silence, a silence that can absorb cries of the heart and in which hopeful
sighs can be lifted up. Such a silence gives words their full
power, whether words of scripture or tradition, or of newspapers or people around us. This silence offers words room to
be heard, to be felt, to be acted upon with a thoughtful
response rather than a mere reaction.

Earlier in his gospel, Mark describes Jesus' busy schedule.
He had just astonished everyone in a synagogue by rebuking
the unclean spirit of a man. Word spread of the incident
throughout the region of Galilee. He stayed with Simon and
Andrew, and healed Simon's mother-in-law from a fever. By
evening, people were bringing to him "all who were sick or
possessed with demons. And the whole city was gathered
about the door" (Mark 1:32–33). By the end of the evening,
Jesus himself must have felt sick with exhaustion, also in
need of healing. So the next morning, "a great while before
day, Jesus rose and went out to a lonely place, and there Jesus
prayed" (Mark 1:35).

Gays and lesbians know a lot about lonely places. The
closet is a lonely place, whether in the midst of a party or of
worship. To encourage us to go to a lonely place to pray
seems redundant to those who are still closeted. To those who
have left the loneliness of the closet, it sounds like a call to
retreat, at least temporarily giving up the community we now
experience. To those who feel lonely in the search for a lover

or friends, the invitation appears to mean more isolation. Yet it was in such lonely places that our sensitivities developed. It was in such places that our awareness grew of suffering in the world.

"Lonely place" in the context of suffering or addressing suffering sounds lonely. But "lonely place" in the context of getting up early to pray suggests privacy. Using the model of lovers for Jesus' relationship with God, Jesus' escaping to a lonely place to pray sounds like a clandestine meeting of lovers. The image suggests intimacy. Given the biblical witness, there is no denying that Jesus enjoyed intimacy with God. He is sent from God, is a child of God (meaning he contains the very essence of God), and those who know him know God. Jesus' expressed wish was that others might know God as intimately as he did. It was this intimacy which offered him peace in a storm.

We Christians have frequently denied ourselves this intimacy with God. We may keep a protective distance. We may be frightened of pursuing a relationship with someone who knows us so well, fearful of exposing those areas of our lives that we believe could affect God's love of us. And we may fear the transformation that love, especially from God, may bring.

Consider how transformed and empowered you have been when you felt loved. Remember my personal example in the chapter on "welcoming embodiment" in which I experienced gratitude and an increased ability to love even those who did not love me, when someone I loved offered me physical affection. Similarly, those whom Jesus healed found themselves changed spiritually as well as physically. The man with the unclean spirit in the synagogue was delivered of that which kept him from giving thanks to God. Simon's mother-in-law was healed and thereby empowered to serve her houseguest. In our own world of unclean spirits, in our own fever-pitched world, Jesus reaches out to touch us, to heal us, to empower us, because he brings us into proximity with God our lover. We are enabled to give thanks to God and to serve God.

As in other relationships, we too often run from One who loves us intimately. Self-doubt, personal insecurity, or cynicism (which is idealism that, disappointed, has turned angry) may cause us to run from God. Jesus did not run. Were it not for his regular rendezvous with God "in a lonely place," how could he have coped with the lonely places to come? Temptations in the wilderness, demands of ministry, struggles with religious and political authorities, forsakenness on the cross—all of these lonely places became opportunities for prayer and occasions for intimacy with God.

As lesbian and gay people, our lonely places may also become opportunities for prayer and occasions for intimacy with God. In my spiritual development, I moved from lonely place to lonely place in search of God and in search of myself. I first believed my homosexuality was both sin and sickness. God did not deliver me from my homosexuality, but did free me from my guilt about my condition. Then I believed my homosexuality was my "thorn in the flesh" or my "cross to bear." I suffered from having feelings that I could not express, let alone fulfill, and believed that this would shape me into a better Christian. God did not deliver me from my feelings, but did free me to accept the gift of my sexuality. When I fell in love with my closest male friend in college, I cried secretly in the closet. God did not deliver me from my love, but did free me from the closet. As I sought to serve the church in the professional ministry, I felt devastated when denied ordination. God did not deliver me from my calling, but freed me for ministry. Throughout my personal history, prayer offered me the perspective to see what God was accomplishing in and through the lonely places of my life.

When I allow it to do so, my prayer life makes me peaceful, connected, gracious, forgiving, and loving—toward myself and others. In God's presence, I more adequately value myself. It may seem paradoxical, but my increasing self-esteem makes me better able to listen to others, to receive criticism, to accept change and compromise. I am better able to recognize the God-given validity of others. My self-worth is less dependent on another's defeat or my victory, less dependent on another's failure or my achievement. Yet, because I value myself, I become less willing to be distracted from the good, the true, and the eternal. My goals make me *stretch* myself rather than *perfect* myself.

Friends of mine who read this self-description will most assuredly advise me to pray more often. "We'd love to see you *more* like this!" they'd chide. And it's true, I have a long way to go toward achieving the integrity God calls me to. *Knowing* what works isn't always *doing* what works.

One day, swimming my usual laps in the pool at the gym, I became immersed in a metaphor of the spiritual life. My swimming feels a little clumsy. My primary goal is to survive rather than drown, which makes my strokes less graceful and causes me to anxiously gasp for air. Here I am, a body which is 60 percent water, afraid of a body that is 100 percent water. And to think I spent nine months immersed in embryonic fluids before I needed to take a breath of air! I thought of a book on swimming which I bought at a church rummage sale but which I have never read, though reading it might improve my style and speed. And I remembered declining a friend's offer to coach me in becoming a better swimmer.

My spiritual life similarly feels a little awkward. Too often I pray only to survive. The nonphysical plane makes me apprehensive, yet maybe 60 percent of me is spirit. Why am I afraid of 100 percent spirit? And wasn't I born of the Spirit in my believer's baptism? I have books—the Bible and various books on prayer—which could teach me to improve my spirituality, but I don't use them adequately. And how well do I really listen to my spiritual advisors, or consult those whom I consider to be spiritual authorities?

Disciple and *discipline* are both derived from a root word meaning "to learn." *Discipline* carries negative connotations for many of us because of commonly employed, punitive-based learning systems. We can overcome whatever aversion we may have to discipline by remembering something we enjoyed learning to do well: skiing, dancing, crossword puzzles, or writing poetry, for example. Each required a discipline, a method of training. To become a better swimmer, I need to follow a certain discipline. So it is for prayer. To develop intimacy with God requires a discipline. As disciples of Jesus, we follow him to a lonely place to pray.

From my experience and reading, I have gleaned some helpful tips on developing a prayer life. One may pray anywhere, but some places are more conducive than others to listening for God's voice in scripture and within one's life experience. Do you have a favorite place in your home, yard, office, or a nearby park where you go to escape and think? That might be the perfect place to pray. It should be available on a regular basis, and a site in which interruptions are unlikely. If the location is indoors, you may wish to "dress the set" by including items which evoke reverence, devotion, and awe. A lit candle, fresh flowers in a vase, a cross hung on the wall, a family Bible on the table—any one of these may increase your openness to prayer.

A regular time when you are most likely to be free of interruptions and to feel the most relaxed about "wasting" time is the best time to meditate and pray. For some people this will be early in the morning before going to work; for others it might be a break during the work schedule; for others, before dinner or late in the day. If it is the same time every day, a rhythm is established. Though daily prayer would be preferable, you may decide to follow a Monday-Wednesday-Friday schedule, or a Tuesday-Thursday-Saturday routine. It's helpful not to schedule too much time per day, because the less time you plan for, the more apt you are to be faithful in fulfilling your commitment. Five, ten, or fifteen minutes would be the quantity of time to begin with. If you miss a time or a day, don't berate yourself, as that will only reinforce any imagined "spiritual inadequacy." Just pick up another time or resume on the next scheduled day. Expect an ebb and flow to your commitment: there may be periods of time when you don't keep to your schedule. Don't worry! Just do what you can, but keep doing it!

If you have a lover or friend interested in sharing this intimate time with you, it may enable you both to keep a disciplined prayer life. It's like having a workout buddy at the gym, encouraging you to work out regularly and to be all that you can be. But you have to be careful to observe a certain period of silence together during your time. You then might describe what surfaced for each of you through meditation on scripture and experience. You may both have to work to keep yourselves on track, avoiding conversation extraneous to the purpose of this time. Others may find a need to be separate, even from a lover, in their prayer life, and no one should feel guilty about this choice. After all, that's how the whole monastic life began!

Music may be helpful during the course of a meditative period, but the rule of thumb is, the more silence, the better! We are bombarded with stimulation throughout the day. This time should be as stimulus-free as possible to allow centering one's heart and mind, and focusing on a few words, read silently or aloud, from scripture or a book of prayers.

Yoga enthusiasts do not have a corner on the knowledge that posture affects thought. Christians have found that standing with upraised arms with eyes open, kneeling with bowed head and eyes closed, and other variations in posture are important for embodying their intentions in a particular prayer. Choose a posture appropriate for you and your intentions in your meditation and prayer. It should be comfortable so as not to be distracting, though not so comfortable that it encourages sleep. I prefer sitting in a chair, resting my hands in my lap, their palms open toward the sky in a receptive attitude. Breathing deeply at a slower rate helps slow us down to become more receptive.

Scriptures (particularly the Psalms, the Prophets, the Gospels, and the Epistles) and books of prayers may serve as conduits between God and your experience. Deeply spiritual people have written these resources as guideposts in developing the spiritual life, that is, a life which recognizes the presence of God in every area of life. But the spiritual life is not necessarily helped—and indeed, may often be hindered—by voluminous reading of these resources. Better to interact with short passages, a few verses that hang together, or a paragraph, so that each reading's message sinks deeply into one's being. Read a passage aloud for content, then read it again, finding a thought, phrase, or word that strikes you as interesting, important, significant, or troublesome at that point in your life. Repeat it over and over again silently, as a kind of mantra, allowing thoughts and feelings to arise in response. If you find yourself wanting to say something to God, do so, but don't rush to speak. Hesitate just in case God has something more to say to you through the particular passage. Father Keating suggests that scriptures serve as topics of conversation in our dialogue with God.

God is steadfast, as our prayer life should be. Persistence is important. There will be periods in your prayer life when you experience God's absence, much like the children of Israel wandering forty years in a barren wilderness, or the lonely desert in which Jesus prayed for forty days. There will be times when our prayer life seems to make little or no difference in the way we relate to the world or the way we experience life. There will be times when our devotional time may lead us to the error of spiritual superiority. And there will also be times (which seem to increase and expand) when we feel centered, anchored, rooted, and at peace even in the midst of storms. We will feel humbled and loved all at once. Healing will occur. Creativity, love, and joy will grow within us, and we will thereby be inspired and empowered.

Periodically, speak about your prayer life with someone whom you recognize as a spiritual authority. Tell her or him where your prayers have led you in your thinking, understanding, and behavior. Describe troublesome aspects, and ask questions. Listen to guidance and advice. For continuity's sake, try to maintain the same spiritual advisor.

Always remember that prayer is never a private act, though it may be personal and individual. That is, whenever you pray, you pray as part of a spiritual community. Rather than being alone in prayer, prayer becomes a way to community with millions of unseen and unknown others who also are directing their thoughts toward God in that moment. When you gain insights through personal prayer, bring them back to your local spiritual community for its edification and creativity. Share them during coffee hour at church, over Sunday brunch, in Bible studies and other church classes, and with the spiritual leadership of the church (whatever form the church happens to take). This, in turn, further shapes and molds our community of faith.

In an Ecumenical Service for Human Rights, which the Lazarus Project helped organize at the Greek Theater in Los Angeles to voice religious opposition to an anti-gay ballot initiative, Peter Yarrow (of Peter, Paul, and Mary) said he believed that acting on behalf of justice was a form of prayer. I believe that it can be. Similarly, prayer may draw us into activities on behalf of social justice. Jesus' lonely place of prayer sensitized and empowered him to recognize and heal the many who suffered injustice: the disabled, the leper, the poor, the disfranchised, and the harshly judged.

The sixth chapter of the Gospel of Mark describes another "lonely place" where the multitudes followed Jesus, and he fed them with a few loaves and fishes. In the lonely place of prayer, Jesus blesses and multiplies the few loaves and fishes we are able to offer. And there is enough for all.

PART III

Discerning Our Call

"For by grace you have been saved through faith; and this is not your own doing, it is the gift of God—not because of works, lest any one should boast," Paul reminded the Ephesians (Eph. 2:8–9). Yet he also told them that Christians are "created in Christ Jesus for good works" (Eph. 2:10), later admonishing them "to lead a life worthy of the calling to which you have been called" (Eph. 4:1) and to "be imitators of God," "walk[ing] in love" (Eph. 5:1–2).

Developing intimacy with God means exposing our dark side to God's redeeming grace, *rising above sin* (chapter 9) not to earn God's welcome home but to rise to the occasion of accepting it. We will learn what *making love* (chapter 10) truly requires in building loving relationships. Loving, as individuals or as the church, may mean *risking the brokenness of the body* (chapter 11), as Jesus was broken on the cross. His political death reminds us that we are called to work for social justice, *crossing politics and faith* (chapter 12).

CHAPTER 9

Rising
Above Sin

Sin is what causes all human beings to stumble on our way home to God's embrace. Sin trips us as we reach out to God's yes to us in creation and in Christ. It may be our own sin, it may be the church's sin, it may be society's. All must be discerned and confessed, not to assure God's already-promised welcome, but to rise to the occasion of accepting it. Discernment of truth is the key to appropriate confession.

We are told by psychology that a person's ability to discern what is true from what is not enables greater mental health and social adjustment. We are told by religion that a person's ability to follow truth and discard what is false means not only spiritual health and well-being, but spiritual growth as well.

Growing up, we were all—gay and nongay—taught a lot of untruths alongside a lot of truths. The untruths were rarely told us for pernicious or malicious reasons. Often they were believed as true by those who taught us and were offered "for our own good": "people of other races cannot be trusted"; "masturbation causes warts"; "parents always know best"; "there is only one way to interpret the Bible." Maturing involves questioning and discarding untruths. Those unable to "put away childish things" find themselves lost in a society in which even truth is challenged. Those who are most lost

83

are considered mentally ill, unable to function and in need of society's care. To challenge them or question their view of the world is to make them anxious, depressed, threatened, and angry.

Most of us discarded enough untruths about the world to allow us to develop realistic worldviews, which in turn enabled us to survive. Psychologically healthy individuals are able, when confronted by truth, to revise their worldviews, their maps of the world, so that their movements through life are informed by greater reality.

Many people who mature psychologically in this way still remain spiritual infants. There must be something in the way the church baptizes its own untruths that makes them the most difficult to question and discard. It's easier for many reared in the church to turn their backs altogether on matters of faith than to confront their doubts and questions. Yet those who appear to us to be giants of the faith are those very people who report and reflect upon their doubts.

People with worldviews which equip them for success in the twentieth century often revert to first-century worldviews upon entering church on Sunday morning. This is not what Jesus meant when he said one should "come as a child." Jesus was talking about coming to him willing to be challenged and to grow. But to challenge many Christians' anachronistic worldviews is to make them anxious, depressed, threatened, and angry. The spiritually ill respond much like the mentally ill who cannot revise their views of the world.

Some so-called successful churches which report phenomenal growth are those which exploit the fact that many Christians want to be assured that everything they were taught as children was true—that, in fact, truth is easily discernible in a handful of spiritual "laws" rather than in daily struggle with doubt, questions, and the discarding of spiritual untruths.

Others may not need their childhood beliefs confirmed, but still believe that simple answers must exist for the most complex spiritual questions. A gay friend recently told me that he wished that after death, someone would set him down in a room and tell him what is true and whom he should follow—whether it is Buddha or Christ or whomever. Then he would accept that and believe and do what he is supposed to. Many people demand that clarity on this side of death. I found my friend's openmindedness commendable, but I felt sad that his need for sure answers seemed to arise from a cynicism about being given so many conflicting answers by the religions in his background.

As gays and lesbians developed psychologically, we questioned the untruths taught us about homosexuality. Our personal experience called into question the dominant, heterosexual culture's viewpoint that everyone was supposed to be straight. The healthier we were, psychologically and spiritually, the better able we were to discern and discard the untruths we had learned about homosexuality. Indeed, one of those untruths was that homosexuality was learned behavior, when, in truth, it is homophobia that is a learned behavioral response, one which we who are homosexual learned alongside our heterosexual counterparts.

As gays and lesbians developed spiritually, we also questioned the untruths the church taught us about homosexuality. Traditional Christian views would have us confess our love as sin, whereas we realized that instead we needed to confess our failure (and the failure of church and society) to affirm our love as sacred. Revising our worldviews was essential to both our psychological and spiritual health, as well as our ability to survive. Of course, doing so challenged the worldview of heterosexist Christians. Those unable to revise their worldviews in the face of truth about homosexuality became anxious, depressed, threatened, and angry.

As a child, I visited my cousins, who lived in a heavily Catholic small town in Kansas. We went to the movies. In the theater, a priest sitting next to me wadded up an empty popcorn bag and beaned a kid with it several rows away. As the boy turned to see who had done it, the priest folded his hands and adopted an innocent, saintly air. The boy then looked at me, and I feared he believed I had been the culprit! Later, during the film, a notice on the screen read: "Concession stand in ten minutes." I was too young to know the word concession, so I confused it with "confession." I anxiously asked my Catholic cousin what the notice meant. I found the ways of this other Christian tradition so mysterious that I considered it possible there might be a public confession time even in a movie house! And my fear was that I would be made to confess a sin I didn't commit, that of the priest's bull's eye. I was relieved when my cousin explained that it meant the refreshment stand would be closing in ten minutes.

My mother taught in a Christian elementary school which I attended. Other teachers' kids and I would often play together waiting for our parents to finish their work after school. A girlfriend and I were playing on the monkey bars, when she fell off and landed on her head. I was helping her up when her mother came out to see what happened. Despite both my friend's and my protestations that it was only an accident, she brought me into a classroom and made me pray to ask Jesus to forgive me for hurting her daughter. Reluctantly, I did so, flushed with embarrassment at the false accusation.

Ron Wesner, a former national president of Integrity, a group in the Episcopal Church for lesbians, gays, their supporters and friends, once gave me one of his poems to read. It was about an art project he had been assigned as a child. After completion, his teacher ridiculed his artwork because he had put blue and green together. "Blue and green do not go together," she had explained. Of course, the irony is that blue and green go beautifully together. The poem reflected on the several ways in life in which he had figuratively put blue and green together, overcoming what he'd been taught. One way was his desire as a man to love another man intimately. Another was his desire to enjoy his spirituality alongside his sexuality. In both cases, he was told such things don't go together. But he found they did go together in each instance, and did so beautifully.

Two lesbian lovers, one Catholic, one Protestant, came to me seeking counsel or referral. They had met as neighbors when both were married, had fallen in love, and realized that two women *could* love each other, contrary to their upbringing. Now they lived together, and in creating a home, were looking for ways to relate better to one another's children. One of the fears that they lived with was that their spouses might seek custody, on the basis that lesbians are "unfit" mothers. Clearly, the intentional way in which they sought guidance for sorting out parental roles made them more fit than many parents.

Lesbian women and gay men have often felt forced to confess sins we haven't committed. Religious leaders have adopted a saintly, innocent air when perpetrating institutional and personal homophobia. Good Christians have assumed the worst about us and insisted we confess sins of which we are not guilty. Heterosexist Christians have insisted a woman with a woman or a man with a man do not "go together." The church has often denied that sexuality and spirituality can go hand in hand. And frequently, former spouses and society have deprived us of our children because religion labels us "morally unfit" as parents.

Our sexual orientation and expression have been condemned as narcissistic, but narcissism is very much in the eye of the beholder. Isn't it heterosexuals who want everyone to be like themselves? Isn't it heterosexuals who have the greater problems with racially mixed marriages? Isn't it heterosexuals who generally expect their children to carry on their traditions, beliefs, and interests?

Our sexual orientation and expression have been condemned as selfish. What is selfish about wanting to love another person, build a supportive gay community, and contribute to both church and society? Isn't it yet more selfish to want everyone to be like you, as so many heterosexuals wish?

Our sexual orientation and expression have been condemned as idolatrous. How can lesbian and gay Christians struggling to worship God within our various traditions despite tremendous opposition be considered idolatrous? It is precisely because we are not willing to make sacrifices on the altar of our sexuality that we are reclaiming our spirituality, our community of faith, our ministry. Through the risks we take in coming out we are making sacrifices on God's altar, as we offer thanks to God for creating us as we are. It is heterosexists who prove idolatrous when they require us to sacrifice God's gifts on the altar of heterosexuality.

What then is our sin? Some Christians have claimed homosexuality is a by-product of the fall of humankind in Adam and Eve's first sin in the garden of Eden. No biblical evidence suggests this. Besides, I believe we need to question the doctrine of original sin, that is, that we are born with a predisposition to sin because of that first sin in Eden. I agree with Matthew Fox, the Roman Catholic theologian, who suggests we need to reclaim our original blessings given to us in Eden. That would at least balance original sin.

Regardless of sexual orientation, to begin our self-understanding with the concept of original sin is like going to bat with two strikes against you. I believe that the primary problem of most people today is lack of self-esteem. The doctrine of original sin reinforces this poor self-image. Here we are, created in God's image, but often our poor opinion of ourselves prevents us from coming home to our spirituality, accepting God's welcome, and receiving our share of God's commonwealth.

And how are we to truly welcome others, value others, and perceive God's image in them, if we don't value ourselves? If we don't value ourselves, other people become distractions to fill our empty lives. To value others is to exchange gifts with them, not simply receive theirs. That means we must have something to offer. To do so means valuing ourselves by affirming our original blessing of having been created in God's image. Lesbians and gays can also affirm our creation in God's image, even if we are reminded by our opposition that we are not specifically mentioned in the garden of Eden story. Remember, factory workers and urban dwellers are also not mentioned in that picture of agrarian bliss, yet they are no less made in the image of God.

Christianity distinguishes between the condition of sin and specific sinful acts. Sin is a condition in which we fail to recognize our dependence on God and our interdependence with one another and all of creation. When we assert ourselves or any person or thing over God, or lord ourselves over others, we commit idolatry. I believe all sinful acts find their root in such idolatry.

Christian faith affirms that Jesus Christ came to redeem us from the condition of sin, this idolatry. As God in human flesh, he embodied what it means to be fully human, that is, made in the image of God. He calls us to return to our original blessings as God's children, heirs of a new heaven and a new earth. His sacrificial life, death, and resurrection restore us to our home with God. Through faith, we may become aware of this and enjoy it.

In his letter to the church at Rome, the apostle Paul was concerned lest the idolatry of the law replace faithfulness to Jesus Christ. In the thirteenth chapter of Romans, Paul sums up the law of God much as Jesus did: "Owe no one anything, except to love one another; for whoever loves one's neighbor has fulfilled the law." Then Paul lists representative commandments from the Law of Moses, claiming they are all summed up in, "You shall love your neighbor as yourself." Paul continues, "For salvation is nearer to us now than when we first believed; the night is far gone, the day is at hand. Let us then cast off the works of the night and put on the armor of the day. Put on the Sovereign Jesus Christ, and make no provision for the flesh, to gratify its desires."

Clearly Paul does not here use "flesh" in the same way as the gospel-writer John does when he affirms embodiment in Christ's nativity, "And the Word became flesh and dwelt among us, full of grace and truth" (John 1:14). And Paul is not echoing Jesus' admonition to have faith that God will provide needed sustenance for our bodies in the pursuit of God's commonwealth.

So we might be tempted to read "flesh" in a limited, erotic way in this and other passages from Paul, largely because that is how it has often been interpreted. But Paul's understanding of "flesh" is different. For Paul, living "according to the flesh" is asserting the transient over the everlasting. Doing so separates us from God. The biblical scholar Günther Bornkamm clarifies this in his book *Paul*.[1] Living according to the flesh is idolizing that in human existence or attitude which opposes or contradicts God and God's Spirit, when that opposition or contradiction is viewed as either the basis or goal of life.

For Bornkamm, this idolatry may find expression in everything from the satisfaction of "gross sensual desire" (which runs the gamut from gluttony to promiscuity) to the religious advantages on which many Christians "base their confidence" (ordination, election to high church office, majority opinion, rigid standards, large churches, big budgets). This means that the church and sexual expression may equally be as much "works of the flesh" as works of God's Spirit. Religion and

sexuality may equally be attempts to assert ourselves in opposition to God and in contradiction of God's Spirit. This is
why Paul can talk about following the law in the same breath
as following sensual desires; both may be ways in which we
gratify the flesh rather than wholeheartedly love God and our
neighbor.

In Romans, Paul addresses the problem of those who assert
themselves over others in following the law. He addresses
himself to the legalistic Christian who idolatrously believes
one can be saved through the law rather than through faith
in Jesus Christ alone. I believe it is the same legalism which
prevents the church from accepting gay and lesbian
Christians today. The claim that salvation depends upon
being heterosexual or behaving heterosexually substitutes a
law for Christ. Such an attitude prevents true love of the
church's gay neighbor.

Though redeemed in Jesus Christ from the condition of
sin, reconciled with God and with one another through his
ministry, we still do not live up to our original blessings as
God's children. That's why the New Testament word for sin
in Greek literally means "missing the mark": *hamartia.* We
miss the mark set for us by virtue of our creation in God's
image. There is no rulebook to follow. In Jesus Christ, we
are freed from a burdening legalism, but called to be responsible to a higher calling: fulfilling the law by loving God and
neighbor. The process of fulfilling our higher calling is called
sanctification. We may stumble in the process, but we know
that God is always present to lift us up, as Jesus did when
Peter began to sink when trying to follow him onto the
stormy waters of the Sea of Galilee.

The reformer Martin Luther believed that loving our
neighbors as ourselves required loving ourselves properly.
Many gays and lesbians have been taught to hate themselves,
having been told so many untruths about that integral part
of their identity: their sexuality. Hating one's self obscures

one's relationships with God and with others. Overwhelmed by shame about who we are, we have trouble relating to God or neighbor. Think of Adam and Eve after their eyes were "opened" and they realized that they were naked. Their shame at their nakedness caused them to hide when God came to walk with them in the cool of the day. Of course, nothing had changed. They had been naked before in their visits with the Almighty. But now they knew shame. This is not dissimilar to the lesbian and gay experience. Our homosexuality preceded the shame we were taught regarding it. It seemed natural until the serpent of homophobia spoiled our innocence. God still came to walk with us, only to find we felt so much shame that we often hid ourselves.

There is a distinction to be made between guilt and shame. When we experience guilt, we are better able to take responsibility for our actions. When we experience shame, our sense of self-worth is so devastated that we cannot begin to own our actions (both right and wrong) because we don't consider ourselves capable of such responsibility. In the garden of Eden, Adam blamed Eve, and Eve blamed the serpent. A person who is ashamed is less likely to change behavior, even when that individual deems the behavior inappropriate.

Many people in the gay and lesbian community act out of shame, behaving irresponsibly to themselves and others. We may abuse ourselves and others: living out stereotypes or viewing others through such caricatures; carelessly and compulsively using drugs, alcohol, or sex to feel better about ourselves; desperately pursuing relationships with abusive or unresponsive partners or becoming abusive ourselves; religiously denying our sexuality and forcing ourselves and others into celibacy or abstinence; defensively rejecting others in exclusive pursuit of masturbation, exhibitionism, or anonymous encounters; flirting with self-destruction or that of others in failing to practice safer sex in the midst of the AIDS epidemic; or discarding a lover or friend out of a fear of intimacy or out of a fear of HIV infection.

These are examples of our dark side that we wish to hide from God out of shame, just like Adam and Eve. Like them, we can blame our actions on the serpent—this time, the serpent of homophobia—rather than take responsibility for them. There's some justification in doing so, since homophobia causes our shame. But, as homophobia is eradicated, and as we grow toward greater self-acceptance in coming home to our spirituality, we must take responsibility for changing our unhealthy coping behaviors, that is, behaviors that negate life and love. We must confess that some of our actions and lifestyle choices did not befit our inheritance as daughters and sons of God. It is time to act responsibly as individuals created and loved by God.

To believe that you are unlovable by God or neighbor is yet another form of idolatry. It asserts that one's self may achieve a state beyond God's reach, beyond God's love. That is not possible in a faith which asserts that God became human, suffered and died unjustly, and descended into the realm of the dead, all that no one may be lost.

If idolatry may be judged by degree, then even more idolatrous are those who assert that *another* person may achieve a state beyond God's reach. And yet that is the position of those who condemn us for being homosexual. The greater idolatry of this position is that heterosexuality supersedes God when heterosexuality is viewed as determining God's response. Only God can determine God's responses.

At the beginning of this chapter, I wrote that sin is what causes us to stumble on our way home to God's embrace. It may be our own sin, it may be the church's sin, it may be society's sin. Homophobia, an irrational fear and loathing of homosexuality and of homosexual persons, makes lesbians and gays stumble on our way home to God's embrace. As such it is sin. It is a sin common to individuals and to every institution within society, including the church. It leads to self-destructive or other-destructive behavior, because it keeps its victim from seeing the image of God in the homosexual person and the Spirit of God in the homosexual experience. It is shared by gays and nongays. Together we must confess it, and allow faith in Jesus Christ to overcome fear of homosexuality. God's yes in Christ must overcome the no of homophobia, because, as Paul also writes, "nothing can separate us from the love of God in Christ Jesus our Sovereign" (Rom. 8:39).

Heterosexism, an exclusively heterosexual worldview, must be corrected by valuing the reality of homosexual persons and perspectives. We must discard the untruth that heterosexuality is a requirement to enter the commonwealth of God. The church needs to repent of its own idolatry: the assertion of the heterosexuality of its majority as the way to God. The church must be called to confess its own "sins of the flesh," its misuse of religious privilege which places it over against God in God's welcome of lesbian women and gay men into Christ's common spiritual wealth.

Speaking to a church about homosexuality, I was asked, "Have you ever considered exorcism?" The person considered my homosexuality to be an unclean spirit. In Jesus' day, spirits were considered unclean when the effect of their presence separated people from the worship of God. The effect of my homosexuality is that it has brought me *closer* to God, as I have become more radically dependent on God's love in the face of rejection by church and society. I believe that I more keenly understand the nature of God's grace than those who more readily enjoy the acceptance of church and society. A charismatic faith healer from the Northwest once told me that, despite the many healings God had wrought through him, he had never been able to change a homosexual orientation. Because he believed God granted the healings to remove obstacles to people's faith, this minister felt led to the conclusion that homosexuality was not such an obstacle.

Both church and society need to be delivered of the twin demons of homophobia and heterosexism, because the effect of their presence separates lesbians, gays, their families, and their friends from the worship of God.

Jesus Christ calls lesbians and gays—and everyone else— not to original innocence, but to our original blessings: created in God's image, loved as God's children, called for God's purpose. God created homosexuality, loves lesbians and gays, and calls us to love one another. Any less of an affirmation than this causes those of us who are lesbian and gay to stumble on our way to receiving God's embrace. Homophobia and heterosexism, whether within us or within the community of faith, trips us as we reach out to God's "Yes in Christ." As individuals and as community, we must confess our homophobia and heterosexism, along with all sins borne of shame, not to assure God's embrace, but to rise to the occasion of welcoming it.

CHAPTER 10

Making Love

"There's more to love than making love," Roberta Flack sang in her hit song "Making Love." The lyrics are all the more poignant because it served as the theme for the film *Making Love* in which a woman realizes she must let go of her gay husband to truly love him. For her, as for everyone, the call of love went far beyond the sexual expression "making love" suggests.

"Making love" may be used as a description of what all love is, in reality: a creation. As all of creation is a gracious gift, so the experience of love is a gracious gift. But, just as humanity was called to be co-creators with God in the creation process, so anyone who receives the gift of love is called to become a co-creator in loving. True lovemaking requires our conscious, creative effort.

"If I give my body to be burned, but have not love, it profits me nothing," the apostle Paul wrote in the famous chapter on love in 1 Corinthians (13:3). Translated to our own time and experience, many of us could testify to giving our bodies, getting burned, and profiting nothing as *we* search for love!

We like to *feel* love. We dream of a knight in shining armor or of an encastled princess. The mythology of romance claims love will come easily, that relationships will be perfect, and that feelings of love last "happily ever after." But our experience of the rest of life is that very little that is worthwhile comes easily, or is perfect, or lasts permanently. It is a difficult lesson, but eventually most learn that love requires hard work, is imperfectly experienced, and has an ebb and flow to its feeling content. Those who don't accept this, or who can't find a partner who does, may become cynical about the possibility of love itself. Because of the lack of opportunities to meet people with whom we have much in common and the societal pressures that destroy rather than uphold same-gender bonding, it's a wonder that more of us are not jaded in this way.

It may be that we, as gay people, hold on to romantic mythology longer than our heterosexual counterparts. One reason is the previous lack of visible role models of gay or lesbian relationships. We don't have enough experience watching same-gender couples working out their relationships together. Another may be the sexually stimulating bar environments which, for many gay men and some lesbian women, have served as a primary socializing source. The fact that we can feel strongly about someone we may meet there might make us think our present partner isn't "the right one," when, in truth, human beings are capable of strong emotional and sexual feelings for many people. And fantasy lovers don't make the mistakes real lovers do!

Finally, a third reason for lingering romanticism may be our hunger for love from a partner to balance the lack of love or expressions of hatred we may experience at the hands of family, people at work, or a prejudiced society. That the love feelings are not always present or are inadequately expressed in our relationship may make us feel we've chosen the wrong partner. The more we grasp that true lovemaking requires effort, forgives mistakes, and includes a spectrum of feelings, the better we are able to accept and embrace a long-term partner.

The love of which Jesus spoke, and indeed the love promoted throughout the New Testament, is just this kind of
love. It is not a love bound by romance, sentiment, idealism,
nor feelings. It is a love that is hard-working, forgiving, and
full of many feelings we don't associate with love, like anger.
Love is a choice that leads us beyond mere feelings. How else
could Christ call us to "love our enemy"? When Jesus commanded that we love God "with all your heart," he meant
we are to love God with all of our *will*, since at that time,
the heart was believed to be the seat of the will rather than
of the emotions. "Love your neighbor as yourself" thus entails *choosing* to love both self and neighbor. The Greek word
used in the text is *agape*, which suggests a benevolent attitude.

Love, for Christians, is a creation of the will more than
an outgrowth of "good vibes." True Christian love enables us
to love even when we don't experience good feelings, even
when we don't feel good, even when the struggle to love
hurts or angers us. Christian love is governed more by choice
than by chance or transient feelings. There's more to love
than *feeling* love.

Scott Peck offers a definition of love which I believe comes
closest to this Christian understanding. Peck is both a psy-
chiatrist and a person of faith who recognizes the need to
integrate the psychological and the spiritual dimensions of
life in any therapeutic process. In *The Road Less Travelled,* he
defines love as "the will to extend one's self for the purpose
of nurturing one's own or another's spiritual growth."[1] This
love is not passive, but active. It requires extending and tran-
scending the self. It is not selfish. Neither is it other-depen-
dent, determined by the other's response or the lover's need
for the other. Its purpose is spiritual nurture, not simply responding to transient or superficial needs, but offering that
which fulfills essential and eternal human needs. The spiritual growth thereby made possible means growth for the *soul*,

an ancient Jewish and Christian concept of life inclusive of both body and spirit.

Recently I witnessed such love at work. Family, friends, and peers gathered around someone they loved who is alcoholic. Risking their relationships with the person, they did an intervention under the supervision of an expert in the field of alcohol abuse. Typical of such therapeutic sessions, they told her of their concern for her well-being, and offered specific examples when her addiction had affected her relationships with them. In many ways, it would have been easier to let her drink herself to vocational ruin and physical death. Several of them did sacrifice intimate friendships, as the woman's defensive anger subsequently shut them out. But she is now beginning a healing process of reclaiming her spirituality through Alcoholics Anonymous. This new community, along with her newfound physical and mental health, is promoting her spiritual growth.

The love dramatically demonstrated in this example is the love which chooses life. Moses set forth God's challenge to all people of faith in Deuteronomy: "I call heaven and earth to witness against you this day, that I have set before you life and death, blessing and curse; therefore choose life, that you and your descendants might live" (30:19). If the Israelites entered into a covenant with God, they would be choosing life for their community. God promised to be with them. They in turn promised to keep the law handed down through Moses, which included the love of God and practical applications of loving their neighbor. God never broke this covenant. But the Old Testament, particularly the prophetic books, deal repeatedly with the many ways in which the people did in fact break their covenant with God.

Through Jesus Christ, Christians also understand themselves to be in a covenant relationship with God. Jesus Christ mediated a new covenant. God promises to be with us in Jesus Christ. In response, we follow Jesus Christ, living by his commandments to love God and neighbor. In this way, Christians choose the abundant life that Jesus promised.

The love relationship between God and us reveals qualities that are essential in the making of love. The first is *covenant*, the making of promises that are agreeable to the concerned parties. Covenants between God and ourselves and covenants between people contain loving and life-giving properties. But, for both Jews and Christians, God's covenant with humanity is not between equals because it is characterized by our ultimate dependence upon God. In contrast, healthy covenants between people are characterized by mutuality and interdependence. As such, they include some degree of compromise and creativity. Gays and lesbians have been creative in establishing such covenants. Necessity is the mother of invention. Men who cannot afford to be identified as gay sometimes enter into covenant relationships which include the mutual agreement not to live together. Women who were married before realizing their lesbian identity may enter into a covenant which allows them to maintain their previous marital and familial agreement. Partners in a heterosexual marriage may agree to one partner's developing a relationship with someone of the same gender in addition to the marriage.

Moralists within *both* the Christian and the gay communities condemn such variations of the marital standard. Some Christians say God ordained marriage between one man and one woman only. Following this model, many gay Christians say homosexuality should be expressed within monogamous relationships. Some gay ideologues say that anything other than exclusively gay relationships is an unhealthy compromise. But we do not live in a neatly ordered world. Without passing judgment on the wide variety of the *forms* of covenant relationships, we would do better to consider their *content*. And it would be better still to examine the content of our own personal relationships rather than those of others. Remember Jesus' admonition to pay attention to the beam in our own eye before looking to the splinter in another's eye. Besides, we know our own motives and circumstances better than those of others.

The broader community has suspiciously viewed the gay and lesbian community's use of the term "lover." To many straights, the word reinforces a perception of promiscuity. In my own writing and speaking, I have often avoided using the word in favor of more acceptable substitutes, such as "partner," "lifemate," "spouse," or "significant other." More recently, I have begun to reclaim "lover." Why should I give up the use of a perfectly good term just because the straight community has given it negative connotations by using it to describe extramarital affairs? And to change our language with straight people underestimates their ability to understand the word in a different context. A man attending one of our Lazarus conferences described himself as initially uncomfortable with the term, until he suddenly realized that *he* was sitting next to *his* lover: his wife!

God's relationship with us models not only its covenant form but also the vital contents of a covenant relationship. The Psalmist praises: "God has remembered God's steadfast love and faithfulness to the house of Israel" (Ps. 98:3). The "house of Israel" could be read as the "house of faith" or the "people of faith." Jewish scripture and tradition repeatedly reveal God's intent to nurture the spiritual growth of the children of Israel as people of faith. Throughout the oppression of Egyptian bondage, the forty years' wandering in the wilderness, the victorious conquest of the Promised Land, the humiliating ouster and exile from their homeland by the Babylonians, God continued to nurture these people of faith. God did so through the liberator Moses, through the gift of the Law, through judges, kings, priests, and prophets. Through these God helped them understand the events of their history within a broader purpose of being a spiritual presence in the world, "a light to the nations." God's love proved steadfast and faithful through it all. So too, our love for another may prove *steadfast* and *faithful* through his or her experiences of oppression, wandering, victory, and exile.

What is steadfast love? It is loyal love—always there, not smothering, not demanding, not always waiting around, but *available*, even when its need is not recognized, even when the need seems desperate, and even when not appreciated, rewarded, or returned. It may become the loyal opposition, but doesn't refuse to engage. It doesn't persist for selfish needs, like a codependent or an addictive personality. It persists for the benefit of the beloved and for the beloved's spiritual welfare. This doesn't mean the expressions of love or the levels of intimacy may not change; it does mean that whatever form it takes, the love remains. It is not dependent on good feelings, for it is a decision of the will. Initial, continuing, or occasional good feelings may accompany and inspire such a conscious or unconscious choice, but it is always a choice. That's steadfast love. And that's how God loves us. God's love challenges us to love others steadfastly.

One of the best human examples of steadfast love in the Bible is found in the relationship of Ruth and Naomi as described in the Book of Ruth. After the death of her sons, Naomi plans to return to her hometown of Bethlehem in Judah. She encourages her two daughters-in-law to remain behind in the land of Moab, their native country. One does ultimately decide to remain among her people, in a familiar culture and religion. But Ruth refuses to be left behind. Her love for Naomi is steadfast enough that she willingly chooses a new country, culture, and religion. Her poetic plea is so beautiful, it is sometimes used in weddings: "Entreat me not to leave you or to return from following you; for where you go I will go, and where you lodge I will lodge; your people shall be my people, and your God my God; where you die I will die, and there will I be buried. May the Lord do so to me [and here she would have made a chopping gesture to her neck or added an unrecorded curse] and more also if even death parts me from you" (1:16–17). Later, other women will say to Naomi of Ruth that she "is more to you than seven sons" (4:15). Gays and lesbians might be heartened that this tender story of steadfast love describes the bond between two of the same gender.

Steadfast love leads to *faithfulness* to the covenant between the lovers. Jewish scriptures speak of the Israelites' faithfulness or unfaithfulness to the covenant with God. When their love wavered, so did their faithfulness to the Law of Moses.

Christians believe the conditions of the covenant with God changed radically in Jesus Christ. Now people of faith were justified not by faithfulness to the Law but by faithfulness to Jesus Christ. The covenant was no longer based in laws and formulas, but based in a divine and human being. That gave the new covenant a living quality the old covenant did not have.

If the nature of the covenant relationship between God and people of faith may be reinterpreted in Jesus Christ, then we surely may reconsider the nature of covenants between people. And surely new human covenants could become *living* arrangements, that is, agreements which do not necessarily adhere to particular forms, laws, or formulas.

Marriage vows, then, may be understood as mutually agreeable promises between lovers. This understanding serves as a basis for the increasing number of couples who choose to write their own wedding vows. One formula does not work for every couple. A formula which works for some couples may not work for all, whether heterosexual, bisexual, or homosexual. Even using the term "couple" may beg the question.

Admittedly, this is dangerous ground. Such a concept flies in the face of our romantic notions, our desire for uniformity, our belief that a certain marriage form was ordained by God. But the concept of marriage changed even within the span

of biblical history. A group in my own denomination which
wants Christians to return to "biblical sexuality" would be
shocked if polygamy and the use of concubines became common practice as in the Old Testament. The group would be
more horrified by Jesus' abandonment of the biological family
(and his encouraging the disciples to leave theirs) in pursuit
of the family of faith and ultimately God's commonwealth!

Monogamy has been the expectation of heterosexual marriages. But this is less commonly expected in the gay community. Are gay couples which are not practicing monogamy
being unfaithful? I believe they are only if monogamy is one
of the mutual promises made to one another. I have witnessed
nonmonogamous, faithful couples. I have also witnessed monogamous couples who are unfaithful to one another in non-
genital ways. They let work, friends, family, or selfish needs
get in the way of their relationship. But because their only
sexual expression is with the partner, they consider themselves to be faithful.

Lest this discussion about monogamy prove offensive to
those sensitive to the AIDS crisis, let me quickly add that I
do believe all ethical choices, including the mutually agreeable promises made by couples, must be life-choosing and
love-choosing, whether for the individual or the relationship
or the community. What was true for the Israelites in choosing between "life and death, blessing and curse" is true for
us today. Safer sexual practices must be employed. Monogamy
is but one of these. And monogamy itself would not be
enough if one partner were infected with HIV; additional
precautions would need to be taken.

Whatever our mutually agreeable promises may be as we
enter covenants, part of being faithful is to be honest about
what we are agreeing to, as well as to be honest when we fail
to live up to our promises and to challenge the other person
when he or she fails to live up to them. Formulating and
keeping our vows grows from and contributes toward our

steadfast love for one another. This is what it means to be faithful.

When the Israelites failed to live up to their promises to God, they atoned for their sins and received God's forgiveness, a forgiveness which restored them as participants in the covenant. For Christians, that atonement is effected in the life, death, and resurrection of Jesus Christ. In Christ, God is sacrificed to effect our reconciliation, our restoration to the covenant. "Greater love has no one than this, that one lay down one's life for one's friends," Jesus said. God is *sacrificially forgiving*. And so we should be. Just before Jesus spoke these words about greater love, he challenged his disciples: "This is my commandment, that you love one another as I have loved you." We are to be sacrificially forgiving, willing to "go the extra mile," willing to "turn the other cheek" by resisting revenge, willing to "forgive them, for they know not what they do."

But this is more than forgiving mistakes and faults. I believe it means adopting an attitude that forgives the lover for not being all we expected or hoped in our fantasies. This is an area in which we are sometimes least forgiving. We may use actual mistakes or faults as excuses to rail against the person who has not lived up to our dreams. For this we must not only seek to "forgive," but seek forgiveness as well.

Sacrifice may lead us one step further. Probably the most difficult issues for lovers to resolve are those of power and control. We are often resistant toward giving up or compromising our power. Jonathan's love for David, described in first and second Samuel, offers an excellent example of this kind of sacrifice. Jonathan was the son of King Saul. He had the right to fight for his father's throne. But, knowing David wanted to be king, he chose to support the man he loved in his quest. Though some biblical scholars have suggested there may have been a sexual relationship between them, what is yet more remarkable to me is Jonathan's willingness to give up power to another man. This was unheard of in his day. And to do so out of love risked "choosing the son of Jesse [David] to your own shame," as his father accused him (1 Sam. 20:30). This model of same-gender love may serve as inspiration to us all in working out the constant compromises covenant relationships require.

There is also an *unconditional* quality to God's love. Jewish prophets heralded the universal aspect of God's love. God's dwelling place was to be "a house of prayer for all peoples." Jesus affirmed this in several ways. He told the story of the Good Samaritan, fully aware that his people thought of Samaritans as an unworthy, mongrel race which worshiped incorrectly. He responded to the faith of the Syrophoenician woman, despite his initial, expected rebuff. He told his disciples that God's rain and sunshine fell "on the just and unjust," then urged them to behave with similar equity: "For if you love those who love you, what reward have you? . . . if you salute only your brothers and sisters, what more are you doing than others?" (Matt. 5:45–47). And, as written of earlier, the early Christians broke once and for all from Judaism when they accepted into their Jewish sect Gentiles who had not first been converted to Judaism. As Peter proclaimed after witnessing Christ's Spirit in them, "Truly I perceive that God shows no partiality, but in every nation any one who fears God and does what is right is acceptable to God" (Acts 10:34–35).

God is not so parochial as we are in showing affection. We are called to broaden our love affair with people. Follow the lead of the Samaritan who helped the wounded stranger. Invite the weary, hungry Emmaus traveler into your home. In offering bread and wine, you may recognize Christ in your midst.

Sometimes it's easier to love the stranger unconditionally than to love our lover or our family or our friends or our fellow Christians unconditionally. After all, we have fewer expectations of the stranger. And there is ego gratification in helping the desperately needy. But we also are called to love unconditionally those whom we know. Otherwise our love may become a subtly manipulative force trying to control other's lives.

Sometimes a lover or friend may try to manipulate us with commands or expectations of unconditional love, regardless of their treatment of us. But only God has the right to call us to love others unconditionally, because only God has unconditionally loved us. There are times when human beings are pushed beyond their limits and are no longer able to forgive sacrificially or to love unconditionally. These are times when we must let God be God and understand that God's love is an ideal that humans may only emulate, not duplicate.

To love unconditionally is always a choice: like being steadfast, faithful, and sacrificially forgiving, loving unconditionally doesn't come naturally. It requires effort. What empowers us to do the "unnatural" is our own experience of God's unconditional love, that unmerited favor, that grace bestowed upon us. This leads to a fifth characteristic of love.

"Beloved, let us love one another: for love is of God, and one who loves is born of God and knows God," says the first epistle to John (1 John 4:7). Our love is *rooted in spirituality:* to love is to be born of God. As we increasingly experience God's gift of love, we too become more gracious. It is like the experience I described in the chapter on welcoming embodiment of being loved one night and feeling loving the following day. It is when we shut ourselves away from God's love that we may find it more difficult to love ourselves and others.

And just as the way to love is found in the way home to God, so the way home to God may be found in lovemaking. Our love blossoms in spirituality: to love is to know God. The lesbian woman who found her spirituality through lovemaking, also described in the embodiment chapter, was beginning to know God. I believe that to choose the spiritual life is to choose to love; to choose to love is to choose the spiritual life.

There is another characteristic of love which we cannot choose because it chooses us. The Psalmist was chosen in this way and celebrates the experience: "Make a joyful noise to the Sovereign, all the earth; break forth into joyous song and praises!" (Ps. 98:4). Love is *energizing*. Whether God's love, the love of a friend, an unexpected expression of love from a stranger, or our own love—all offer us a vitality, a joy, an excitement, a fulfillment, and an inspiration.

Making love is about making choices: to covenant together, to be steadfast, to be faithful, to be sacrificially forgiving, to love unconditionally, and to choose the spiritual life which serves as both inspiration and fulfillment of this love. It is conscious choice and hard work, but then love's energizing quality chooses us. Making love is choosing life, and the abundant life Jesus promised us.

CHAPTER 11

Risking the Brokenness of the Body

To reach out in love is to risk being hurt. Before a gay person knew there were others like himself or herself, to reach out in love was to risk being destroyed. Even now, as we are aware of others like ourselves and have found some sense of community, to reach out in love is to risk losing family, friends, church, job, and reputation. Our survivor's tenacity makes it difficult to hear a call to vulnerability. Yet many of us have truly lived Jesus' words, "One who saves one's life will lose it, and one who loses one's life for my sake and the sake of the gospel's will save it" (Mark 8:35). Others have remained so tightly in the closet that they have not risked love, and, like the rich, young ruler whom Jesus told to sell his possessions and distribute the money to the poor, these have walked away sorrowful, rich in closets.

A column I wrote about the hesitancy of many closeted gay clergy to be supportive of gay Christians prompted a closeted church leader to ask me what he could do to help our cause within the church. He had considered confiding his homosexuality to a close friend of his who was also a high-ranking church official, one who had been our opponent in many national governing councils. He felt his coming out to him might soften his negative stance. I agreed that it could be helpful. After he revealed his homosexuality and received

109

a personally affirming response, his supportive wife wrote me
to express her anger toward me for encouraging him to do so.
Essentially she told me that I didn't know what I was asking
him to do, what risks he was taking for both of them in this
self-disclosure.

It is true that those of us who have already endured the
birth pangs of coming out may have forgotten the pain we
experienced in that process, just as we have forgotten the
pain of our biological births. It is also true that coming out
is more painful for some than for others and extends to significant others who suffer alongside. In combat, military leaders frequently prefer young recruits, because they take more
risks, are less likely to consider what there is to lose, and
indeed, often are believed to have less to lose than older men
and women who have already established themselves. The
battle for gay rights has relied more heavily upon the young
for similar reasons. Still, it is not easy for them either.

Counseling many who are in various stages of this birth
process, I have often been reminded of the depths of terror
faced by those for whom coming out as a gay person will be
the most challenging event of their lives. It may truly be a
born-again experience in which a person dies to old self-
understandings and expectations, to be born into new understandings and perspectives. Like any conversion process,
coming out continues throughout a lifetime. But there are
points along the way in which coming out becomes dramatic:
coming out to one's self, coming out to the family, coming
out at work, coming out at church, and so on.

In her foreword to my book *Uncommon Calling*, Virginia
Ramey Mollenkott writes that self-disclosure is never a moral
imperative. I understand her reasoning, as well as the pastoral
dimension of her assertion. I also appreciate the political advantage of nondisclosure in terms of subversion, that is, closeted gays and lesbians being able to accomplish far more for
our cause than they would be allowed to if they were public
about their sexual orientation.

But, spiritually speaking, I have reservations. In a book of essays by various authors entitled *Is Gay Good?*, Henri Nouwen, a writer on spiritual concerns, maintains that the homosexual person needs to be available to his or her feelings in every context—only then can one's sexual identity be fully integrated into every aspect of one's life so that it may take its proper place within one's fuller identity.[1] I strongly agree and believe that availability to our identity in every possible context contributes to our spiritual well-being.

I believe there is a second step to be taken. Christian compassion has called us into identification with all who suffer. Remember the story of the Last Judgment in which Jesus commends the saints: "I was hungry, and you gave me food, I was thirsty and you gave me drink, I was a stranger and you welcomed me, I was naked and you clothed me, I was sick and you visited me, I was in prison and you came to me" (Matt. 25:35–36). And think of Esther, mentioned earlier, who, though gaining power and privilege in the king's court, risked it all to reveal her ethnic identity to protect her people from annihilation. This identification with those who suffer is also a part of our calling. To some degree, identification with gays and lesbians who suffer *demands* self-disclosure.

Jesus said, "Let the children come to me, and do not hinder them; for to such belongs the kingdom of heaven" (Mark 10:14). What about gay children? Doesn't the lack of visible gay adult Christians hinder their coming home to Jesus? Consider too those described by Paul as infants in Christ: adults newly converted or nominally Christian, both undeveloped in Christian faith. Those who are lesbian and gay need models of the integrity of that faith and their sexuality. And what of lesbian women and gay men outside the faith, who might be attracted to Jesus Christ if they knew he has already welcomed people like them?

There is yet another aspect of self-disclosure. The German theologian Dorothee Solle once shocked me in a speech on nuclear disarmament by saying, "I would rather be among the

killed than among the killers." The statement shook my survivor's mentality to its core. "No!" I thought to myself, "I
would want to survive." But as I meditated on her words, I
understood her spiritual truth. She was admonishing us not
to let fear—in this case, fear of nuclear war—change our
nature from that of a civilized society to that of murderers.
One might consider this in relation to terrorism or the death
penalty as well. I considered the transforming dynamic of fear
in relation to what the closet makes of us. It isolates rather
than unites us. It smothers rather than celebrates who we
are. It makes us liars instead of lovers, cynics instead of ro-
mantics. It makes us less of a community than we could be,
less of a person than we are. I believe we must not let the
closet keep us from being everything God created us to be.
Our call, as Jesus cried to Lazarus in his tomb, is "Come
out!" Unfortunately, many of us will prefer to rest in peace.

The church also prefers to rest in peace. Recently, speaking to a church group, someone asked me if the church's
reluctance to welcome gay people grew more from negative
feelings or from inertia. I admitted it was probably caused
more by the inertia of the church, its inability to shift its
course. Negativity toward homosexuality is there, homophobia is present, but the real problem is that the church is
becoming more of a closet-tomb which suppresses abundant
living and more of a doctrinal museum fearful of current experience.

I occasionally take personal retreats at an Episcopalian retreat house overlooking Santa Barbara. Mount Calvary is run
by the Order of the Holy Cross. As one might suspect with
names like that, there are many depictions of Jesus on the
cross in sculptures, carvings, and paintings. One stormy afternoon, sharing pizza and wine in front of a cozy fireplace, one
of the brothers and I discussed the ramifications of the relatively recent decision of the Episcopal Church in the United
States to ordain women. I was surprised that, despite his

liberal views, he opposed women's ordination. He did so not because he opposed it per se, but because it would interfere with any hope of reunion between the Anglican and Roman Catholic communions. "I'd have no problem with it if Rome ordained women," he explained.

I considered the many similar objections to the ordination of lesbians and gays in my own Presbyterian Church. The impending reunion of the United Presbyterian Church in the U.S.A. and the Presbyterian Church, U.S., which had split over the abolition of slavery one hundred years earlier, might have been impeded if the more liberal northern congregations had approved ordination of homosexuals. So the constant cry that ordaining homosexuals would split the church was sounded even more to muster our defeat. (I believe the church would do more to keep its dwindling fold if it banned ordination of boring preachers and belligerent clergy!)

Also fresh in my mind were the recent concerns expressed over the unity of the National Council of Churches in the United States, if it accepted the membership of the predominantly gay Universal Fellowship of Metropolitan Community Churches.

As I considered all these perceived threats to the church as the Body of Christ, I reflected on the many images of Jesus on the cross in the retreat center. Repeatedly reminded of the brokenness of our Lord, a response to the brother who opposed women's ordination came to me. I rhetorically asked him, "When Jesus was faced with the choice of doing what was right or keeping his own body from being broken, which did he choose?"

Paul wrote to the church at Philippi that Jesus "did not count equality with God a thing to be grasped, but emptied himself, taking the form of a servant, being born in our likeness. And being found in human form he humbled himself and became obedient unto death, even death on a cross" (Phil. 2:6–8). "He learned obedience through what he suffered," affirms the epistle to the Hebrews, which some biblical scholars assert may be the only book in the Bible written by a woman (Heb. 5:8). But, she explains, "In the days of his flesh, Jesus offered up prayers and supplications, with loud cries and tears, to him who was able to save him from death, and he was heard for his godly fear" (Heb. 5:7).

This is clearly a different vision of God than the Almighty presented in the Old Testament. This is a God who, out of sacrificial love, leaves the closet of heaven to descend to earth and become like us, "tempted in every way as we are," willingly living and working among us and dying at our hands—all to bring us God's Word of love (Heb. 4:15). This is a deity who risks the brokenness of the body to call us home to God.

Many Christians feel uncomfortable with this image of God. They want to believe that God is all-powerful as well as all-loving. Our imperfect world belies the possibility that God is both. If God is both, God may be blamed for either causing or allowing human suffering. In his book *The Divine Relativity*, process theologian Charles Hartshorne suggests that, facing a contradiction between an all-loving yet all-powerful God, it would be better to sacrifice our understanding of God as all-powerful than to sacrifice our understanding of God as all-loving.[2] We conceive of God as the best possible entity, and when we think of the best possible person we know, we are more likely to choose the most loving over the most powerful. Even the Superman hero in comic books is not attractive because he is super powerful, but because he uses his super powers for good, in other words, lovingly.

For many years I found this reasoning worked for me. But then it occurred to me that perhaps our understanding of power was distorted, for we think of power in terms of possession and control. In my own loving experiences, I found that my attempts at possession and control had nothing to do with love, nor did they bear any resemblance to the spiritual power I witnessed in others whom I considered more mature in faith. In his temptations in the wilderness, Jesus' response to the Tempter's offering him possession and control of all the kingdoms of every age on earth was, "Begone, Satan! for it is written, 'You shall worship the Lord your God and God only you shall serve'" (Matt. 4:10). Possession and control do not characterize God's power. Love is God's power. Possession and control is worldly power, love is spiritual power. Process theology understands God as one whose love is persuasive rather than controlling. Biblically there is much basis for that perception. God leads us as a shepherd, challenges us in a prophet, models human life for us in Jesus Christ, influences us as a teacher, empowers us like a counselor, and inspires us as the Spirit.

When I was finishing my first book, Uncommon Calling, I took my typewriter and my manuscript to Mount Calvary for two weeks. Here I worked on the final chapter, recounting the painful defeat of efforts to obtain ordination of gays and lesbians in my denomination and describing the meaning of that defeat for me. As I wrote, I found deeply buried grief and pain and anger resurrected within me. Also, the knowledge that I had yet to find a publisher for my book haunted me. I wondered if anyone even wanted to hear my story. I took my many feelings into my prayer life during my working retreat, praying for understanding, for resolution, and for healing from these overpowering and painful feelings.

I began to look more intently at the crucifixes on the walls in Mount Calvary, especially the one carved of wood in the chapel. Monasticism has deeply influenced my spiritual life, but I had formerly maintained a Reformed dislike for the contemplation of Christ's suffering on the cross. Those who contemplate it are likely to duplicate it, it had seemed to me. And I offered hearty Protestant applause to those who avoided crosses and lived "Easter lives," or, better yet, to those who took action that removed the crosses of others so that they might live out the resurrection.

Reviewing and editing my manuscript, my book seemed to me to be filled with crosses for myself and others. I had enjoyed my life, my ministry, and even the church. Why did the cross overshadow my joy? Perhaps I had avoided contemplating crucifixes because I had witnessed too many crucifixions of lesbian and gay Christians in the church.

During one morning's Eucharist, as Christ's body was broken and Christ's blood was spilled *again*, I looked toward the figure of Jesus on the cross above the sacrament. What I witnessed at that moment may prove offensive to some: instead of simply seeing a limp and lifeless body, I saw One who was *relaxed*. The goodness of the crucifixion dawned on me. Jesus surrendered his will to God's. He trusted God. I thought of my own spiritual need to relax, trust God, to be loving rather than controlling. If God can make sense out of Jesus' suffering and render him the victor, then gay Christians may take hope that our suffering is not in vain. We can fulfill our prophetic ministry, no matter what others may do to us. Our crucifixion is *their* last resort, not God's.

Every closet and every church needs a crucifix. It's time for lesbian and gay Christians to contemplate Christ's suffering, for it reminds us that God suffers with us. It's time for Protestants to get those bodies back on our pretty, empty crosses, for it will link us to the suffering of those who are being crucified today. It's time for all Christians to take seriously that the church as the Body of Christ must continually risk the brokenness of that body to do what is right.

I believe that Jesus on the cross calls lesbian and gay Christians to risk the brokenness of our bodies, in order to fulfill a prophetic ministry with the church. I believe that

Jesus on the cross calls the church to risk the brokenness of its body to fulfill its pastoral ministry with gays and lesbians. Our Christian faith assures us that, no matter how difficult it will be, fulfilling these calls leads to resurrection.

CHAPTER 12

Crossing Politics and Faith

I believe that Jesus on the cross calls us not only to fulfill a prophetic ministry and to create an inclusive church, but also to reform society.

Watching the 1988 Democratic National Convention, I thanked God that I had lived long enough to see John Kennedy, Jr., introduce his Uncle Teddy. I remembered only too well John-John's heart-rending salute to his fallen father a quarter of a century before.

Americans are no strangers to political tragedies. From assassinations to resignations, from disfranchisement to apathy, great causes have suffered at the hands of everything from mentally unstable individuals to tyrannical majorities. The lesbian and gay movement is also familiar with this experience: Metropolitan Community Churches and gay centers have been bombed or burned; Harvey Milk, famed gay city supervisor in San Francisco, was assassinated; lesbian and gay rights have been defeated by popular vote and gubernatorial vetoes; and violence against us has increased.

Now AIDS looms on our political horizon. My experience in the church is that AIDS has opened heretofore closed doors. But political activists warn of a backlash. Decriminalization and civil rights take back seats as we protect the rights of persons with AIDS and seek governmental funding that is adequate to the tasks of education, treatment, a vaccine, and hopefully, a cure. Voters' ballots and legislatures' dockets of recent years have included measures to quarantine or otherwise control those who may be infected with HIV. We may be in the midst of yet another political tragedy, a tragic end to the promise of gay and lesbian acceptance. What can people of faith do about this potential political tragedy? Or any political tragedy?

Social gospel advocates urged Christians to become involved in politics in the '60s. By the '80s, the religious right was commanding its ranks to get involved. Both decried the other's initiative. But both were correct in bringing their faith into politics.

After all, Jesus' struggle for our spiritual conscience had political ramifications. As a result, two millennia of Christians have been confronted, whenever entering a church, with a political tragedy: the cross. In Jesus' day, a religious heretic would have met death by stoning. But crucifixion meant a political martyrdom at the hands of Rome. The death of Jesus Christ was political. I believe it was God's way of identifying with our political suffering and calling us, in love, to risk the brokenness of our bodies by doing what is right for the body politic.

Some Christians say that people of faith don't belong in politics. But if the story of the Gospel—culminating in the greatest political tragedy of all time—does not prick your conscience and get you involved in affecting the conscience of this nation and the world, then the incarnation of God's will for this world ends with the cross.

The connection, the tie that binds, the bond which weds politics and faith, is the cross. Political tragedy occurs when life is destroyed or denied, whether is be the life of an individual, a people, or a social justice movement. Faith comes into play because the valuing of God-given life is the concern of faith. Consequently, anything which interferes with life and its fullness is what faith must adamantly oppose, whether bullets, missiles, hunger, toxic wastes, acid rain, drug abuse, inequitable distribution of the world's goods, inadequate health care, or the denial of human rights.

To update an old illustration of Christian political action: A person is suffering with AIDS. Christian compassion requires caring for that individual and ministering to the person's lover and family. But equally a part of our ministry is the political action required to determine why government has been so slow to respond to the AIDS epidemic and to find ways to correct the problem.

For Christians, faith must take precedence over politics. Politics cannot be allowed to control, limit, or paralyze faith, whether it be politics within society or politics within the church. God's higher law must reign supreme for the Christian. In this regard, we need to pray for the gift of discerning the spirits, for there are demonic forces which would baptize a particular political ideology as *the* Christian stance. This is the heresy of the religious right. To claim that Jesus would endorse deployment of an MX missile is ludicrous. To believe that Jesus would wholeheartedly endorse the conservative agenda is simply not credible. And to think that Jesus would approve of depriving lesbians and gays of basic human rights is at odds with his own lifestyle of spending time with the outcasts of society.

But liberals have our own tendency to claim an exclusive, divine right for our views. The West Hollywood Presbyterian Church prided itself on being a liberal-to-radical enclave within an often conservative denomination. After I led a church membership course one spring, a participant took me aside to tell me that he was not sure if he belonged in our church. Thinking it was some disagreement with the tenets of our faith or polity, I asked him why. He startled me with his reply, "Because I'm a Republican!" I laughed, a little embarrassed, and quickly explained that we *did* have Republican members, and that he would be most welcome to join! I am glad to say that he did.

I do believe that Christian political action must be characterized by choosing life and taking compassionate action for those who suffer. Any policy which would ignore suffering, or disfranchise, exploit, or kill, should be anathema to the Christian. Any policy whose goals are justice and mercy reflects to a degree the nature of God's commonwealth. Clearly, such a policy may be bipartisan. And my experience has taught me that attitudes toward gay and lesbian issues do not neatly differentiate along liberal-conservative lines. Indeed, I've been most disheartened by *liberals* who refuse to embrace our cause.

Responding to the AIDS crisis may serve as a litmus test for discerning such life-choosing and compassion in politicians and policies. By common political standards, it may be expedient for tens of thousands of gay men, intravenous drug users, women, babies, hemophiliacs, and racial minorities to die due to an inadequate governmental response to AIDS. But by Christian political standards, I believe it stinks in the nostrils of God as much as the expedient nature by which another government disposed of Jesus.

To ensure that we do not claim an exclusive, divine authority for our political viewpoint and to integrate our politics and faith, our quest for justice must be accompanied by grace and mercy. Though collectively Christians serve as the Body of Christ, none of us individually can claim the authority of Jesus. And each of us must be careful not to become enslaved to a particular ideology that inhibits the free movement of the Holy Spirit within us and within our community of faith. "For freedom Christ has set us free," Paul wrote the Galatians, "do not submit again to the yoke of slavery" (Gal. 5:1). Paul was warning Christians not to fall back into any new kind of legalism.

The closet is a form of slavery for gay people. The church has come to represent legalism to gays and lesbians. Too many of us escaping the closet or the church quickly run to a new form of slavery and legalism. Too readily we agree with those who tell us not to waste our time on the church. Too readily we might dismiss our own spirituality, our own Christian faith. Too easily we might embrace a new ideology that celebrates our sexuality at the expense of our spirituality. Too easily we might become so "ideologically correct" that we cannot listen to those that we believe are not.

In 1978, I persuaded the Los Angeles Gay and Lesbian Religious Coalition and several nongay ecumenical religious groups to cosponsor an Ecumenical Service for Human Rights, in order to voice religious opposition to a California ballot initiative. Proposition 6, sponsored by state senator John Briggs, would have led to the firing of schoolteachers who were either gay or who advocated gay civil rights. The religious right actively campaigned for the initiative, and, lest voters believe that the religious right was the only or the predominant religious viewpoint, the No on 6 campaign strategists believed that an event drawing public attention to more tolerant religious viewpoints would help defeat the proposition. The primary responsibility for organizing the worship service fell on the shoulders of gay religious groups. We put a lot of work and money into the project. It was both spiritually meaningful and politically successful, and, just two days before the election, drew media attention to more positive religious attitudes toward gay rights. It contributed to the defeat of the dangerous initiative.

After the glow of this victory, however, I felt devastated to see how a local gay paper reported the event under the headline: LET US PREY. The writer, obviously exercising a personal vendetta against religion, attacked the worship service as an attempt to evangelize gays and lesbians on behalf of religion. That the event was organized by lesbian sisters and gay broth-

ers made no difference. The writer's ideology made him blind
to our contribution to the community's struggle against an
oppressive political move.

Affirmation, the gay Methodist group, held its national
gathering one year at the West Hollywood Presbyterian
Church. Many in attendance during the weekend meeting
chose to worship with our congregation on Sunday. Reverend
Dick Hetz, who led services once a month, was in charge of
the liturgy that day. Dick made the mistake of using as a
responsive reading a Psalm straight from the hymnbook, a
Psalm which contained frequent references to God and humanity using male personal pronouns. Some attending the
worship service from the visiting group walked out in protest
of the noninclusive language. Others who had worshiped
with us before and knew of our usually inclusive language,
remained with us.

A few weeks later, Dick explained to me how surprised he
himself had been as he was leading the Psalm. When he had
last used it twenty years ago, before he was forced to resign
as pastor of a Presbyterian church because he was gay, nobody's consciousness was sufficiently raised to notice the exclusively male language. He felt sad and apologetic about the
episode.

The night after he expressed these concerns to me, Dick
Hetz was murdered. A man whom he had met and invited
home to dinner used the offered hospitality as an opportunity
to rob him. Tying him up at gunpoint, the guest then slashed
his throat and later fired a bullet into his head. The tragic
loss of this pastoral figure was to reverberate through our
congregation for years. Here was a deeply sensitive, spiritual
man whose life was snatched away by the violence to which
members of our community are so vulnerable when reaching
out for love.

The ones who walked out of the worship service that Dick
conducted forever missed out on the spiritual insights one

who had suffered for our mutual cause may have offered in his sermon. Unmercifully and ungraciously, these guests had judged him to be "politically incorrect," and they, I believe, left spiritually incomplete.

No matter how good or godly we believe our ideologies to be, unless they are accompanied by mercy and grace, they become as "sounding gongs or clanging cymbals." In choosing friends, I do not feel comfortable around those with whom I have to be constantly on guard lest I prove ideologically incorrect. I look for friends with whom I can kick back, get off the soap box (and have them get off theirs), and even be inconsistent in applying my political, religious, and social viewpoints. I'm not talking about friends who allow me to be hypocritical, but friends who trust that my heart is in the right place, even if I make an ideological mistake. I want friends who don't go into a rage, write me off, or cry how much I've hurt them or the cause by an unintentional political blunder. I want to feel at home with my friends.

I believe this dynamic is a contributing factor in the divisions lesbian women and gay men experience. Perhaps because of their double experience of oppression as both women and lesbians, many lesbians are more politicized than their gay male counterparts. Many lesbians are therefore more sensitized to nuances of oppression. Whereas gay men frequently deflect or perhaps deny oppression with an outrageous sense of humor, lesbian women often feel oppression deeply. Gay men may complain that lesbians are "too serious," and lesbians may complain that gay men are not serious enough. As we accept one another's gifts more graciously and learn from one another, I believe these divisions will be overcome. We need a merciful, gracious freedom within the gay community when it comes to matters of political ideology.

I believe we need this merciful, gracious freedom in the church as well. When I was at Yale, Professor William Muehl from the Divinity School preached at Battell Chapel on the main University campus. As his sermon began critiquing the feminist movement and then attacked the gay liberation movement, I stormed out in protest. I startled him, because I chose to exit a side door not far from his pulpit rather than leave by way of the front door of the church. Afterward I realized that I should not have allowed our difference to keep me from the body and blood of Christ offered that day in the observance of Communion. Nor should I have allowed it to keep me from sharing that body and blood with him.

Years later, Bill Muehl sent me a brochure describing a luncheon series planned by the Gay/Straight Coalition at Yale Divinity School. "I thought you might be interested in where your early gay activism has led," he wrote in his friendly letter. When I returned to the campus ten years after my graduation, we were able to laugh about my earlier sudden departure from worship. "I've always wanted to ask you," he began, "why on earth did you go out that door right by the pulpit?" "Because, since I was sitting in one of the front pews, it was the closest one," I replied, "and I didn't want to make too dramatic an exit by walking all the way back down the center aisle!" It felt like coming home, being able to have our differences, respect each other's good intentions, and laugh about our expressions.

Most of us are tempted to attribute the worst motives to our opponents. People who seem the most patient often attribute the best motives to their opposition. The truth is probably somewhere in between, but the advantage of attributing positive motives to opponents is that we may then better understand how they view their opinions. We are also reminded that people frequently hold incorrect views for very good reasons. We might remember that the people who crucified Jesus were good people with good reasons for their action—or so they thought! To attribute the worst motives to an opponent may lead to angry confrontations, making resolution difficult, since proving ourselves right depends too much upon making the other person wrong.

This doesn't mean we accept the opinions of others when we believe them wrong. But we challenge their opinions with the knowledge that even if they're wrong, they stand in the same grace that we enjoy should *we* be wrong.

Someone I was dating invited me to attend the ten-year reunion of his high school graduating class. We were the only gay couple in attendance, although we noticed gay individuals there with straight dates. The emcee of the event, a former football hero, offered an opening monologue during the program. Toward the end, wanting to gain applause in his departure from the podium, he said, "Don't you understand? If you're not Communist or queer, I want you to applaud." Neither my date nor I applauded. I leaned over to him and said, "I notice you're not applauding." "That's because I'm a Communist," he joked dryly.

During a break in the proceedings, I surprised myself by boldly approaching the emcee and telling him my objection to his comment. Using a cliché I'd never used before nor ever used since, I explained my objection by saying, "I'm gay and I'm proud." Flustered and apologetic, he admitted it was "a mindless thing" for him to say. I added that I understood he didn't mean for it to come out that way, but that he had nonetheless offended a number of gay people attending the affair. I felt pleased, because I had challenged him without making him a bad person in my own mind.

The political practice of "passive resistance," used both by Mahatma Gandhi and by Rev. Martin Luther King, Jr., was based on the principle that oppressors could be people of conscience doing bad things. They could be shamed by their own violent reactions toward the oppressed who practiced noncooperation with unjust systems and civil disobedience of unjust laws. At least the broader society and world could be shamed into responding on behalf of the oppressed.

Though passive resistance has been and can be employed by gays and lesbians, the difficulty in translating it into our movement lies in the fact that our oppressors already express violent reactions toward our very existence, independent of and *a priori* to any resistance we may offer. Resistance, then, is perceived as revolution rather than reform, since simply coming out of the closet may invite violent reactions. Whether such violent reactions lead to shame in those who experience them depends on their love for the individual taking that risk. Whether the violent reactions lead to shame in others who witness them depends on how deeply homophobia affects their judgment. Homophobia is as pervasive and powerful as racism and sexism, but its expression is least often challenged. It will require much risking of brokenness in order to overcome it. Only then will political reform occur.

I began this chapter by mentioning a highlight of the 1988 Democratic National Convention. Another, more far-reaching highlight for me was seeing Rosa Parks enter the convention hall on the arm of the first serious black candidate for the presidency, Reverend Jesse Jackson. She was the black seamstress who, in refusing to give up her bus seat to a white passenger, fanned the flames of an already-kindled black civil rights movement in the '50s. She is testimony that one person *can* make a difference in risking the brokenness of her body to promote political justice. And she had lived long enough to see this Easter moment for her people, when a black man could be a serious contender for the nation's highest office. May we in the lesbian and gay movement live so long.

PART IV

Making Our Witness

Gay and lesbian Christians could paraphrase Paul in the third chapter of Ephesians: "When you read this you can perceive our insight into the mystery of Christ, which was not made known to previous generations as it has now been revealed to us, Christ's holy apostles and prophets by the Spirit—that is, how lesbians and gay men are fellow heirs, members of the same body, and partakers of the promise in Christ Jesus through the gospel.

"To us . . . this grace was given, to preach to gay people the unsearchable riches of Christ, and to make *all* see what is the plan of the mystery hidden for ages in God who created *all* things."

Making such a witness will be perceived as *turning the church upside down* (chapter 13). *Opening blind eyes* will challenge modern-day Pharisees who proclaim AIDS as God's punishment for homosexuality (chapter 14). The gay Christian movement is *manifesting Christ's glory*, from nativity to resurrection (chapter 15). Bringing the good news of the Gospel to lesbians and gays requires a fresh understanding of *evangelizing* (chapter 16).

Turning the Church Upside Down

Some years ago I spent a week leading workshops and doing media interviews as the guest of the First Presbyterian Church of Fort Wayne, Indiana. Toward the end of my stay, a woman from the church sponsoring my visit told me a dream she had during my stay. In the dream, she stood with other parishioners beside the massive church buildings of the First Presbyterian Church. For some unknown reason, the others had decided to pull down its tall steeple, and had lassoed it with long ropes. The whole structure groaned and grumbled from the strain as they pulled and tugged at the ropes encircling the steeple. The building looked as if it might cave in at any moment.

Panicked, the woman telephoned the pastor to find out what to do. But the pastor, out calling on other parishioners, was unavailable to offer guidance. The woman returned to the scene just in time to witness the steeple topple to the ground. After the steeple fell, the rest of the church collapsed, and all was destroyed.

Still in her dream, the woman turned from the terrifying scene and found herself walking arm-in-arm with her best female friend from college. In that instant, she realized that the church which had been destroyed was not the First Pres-

byterian Church of Fort Wayne, but rather, the church she
had attended while in college.

On my flight home from Fort Wayne, I reflected on the
woman's interpretation of her dream. The dream, she was
certain, was related to my visit, since it had to do with her
desire for physical intimacy with another woman, as well as
her fear that such intimacy threatened the church. Her ability to accept this intimacy with a woman in the dream was
preceded by the downfall of the church, but not her current
one; rather, it was the church of her youth. The sure answers
of her youthful faith, which precluded homosexuality, were
threatened by my witness that one can be gay and Christian.
Along with most church members, the potential integrity of
homosexuality and Christianity seemed to turn the church
upside down for her.

"Those who have turned the world upside down have come
here also" (Acts 17:6). That statement came from the leadership of organized religion in the days of the first Christians.
The religious authorities voiced it about the early church,
which they perceived as turning the beliefs and practices of
the world upside down. The sect included uncircumsized
Gentiles, recognized women in leadership roles, and held
possessions in common. The sect's leaders preached faithfulness to Jesus Christ rather than to the Law of Moses. It
preached the heresy that God had been embodied in human
flesh. And the Christian movement found its earliest roots
among the poor, the illiterate, and the rural, contrasted with
the wealthy, educated, and urban religious establishment.
The gospel of Christ, heard largely by the dispossessed, became a potential medium for societal and spiritual revolution.
Small wonder that the religious leaders of Thessalonica complained to city authorities about the visiting Christian evangelists, saying, "Those who have turned the world upside
down have come here also."

Little did I know that when I affirmed my homosexuality within the context of my Christian faith and within my community of Christian faith, I would receive the same frightened reaction from other Christians. I did not think of myself as a revolutionary, yet I found myself immediately branded "an avowed, practicing homosexual" at the forefront of "a homosexual lobby" intent on bringing "the sexual revolution" into the church. I never considered homosexuality a philosophy to be "avowed," as one might avow being a Communist or a Christian. I simply *affirmed* that God created me gay. The term "practicing" implied promiscuity rather than the committed, loving relationship I hoped for. Bill Silver, whose candidacy for ordination to the ministry brought the issue to the Presbyterian Church on a national level, used to say that, instead of describing himself as a "practicing" homosexual, he much preferred to think of himself as *accomplished!* After all, he had been in a relationship for five years.

What was perceived as "a homosexual lobby" was a handful of gay men and lesbian women, alongside a few friends, family members, and supporters, who hoped to bring healing to gays and lesbians wounded by the church, and who sought to bring reform to the church's ministry so that it might include a compassionate outreach toward them. Our intent was not subversion, as our opposition asserted, but conversion. Yes, we had benefited indirectly from the so-called sexual revolution, in that it had created a more tolerant societal milieu for our emergence. But no, we were not advance troops in a carefully organized new front for that sexual revolution. The sexual revolution never lent itself well to such organization and control anyway, because it was a reaction to an oppressive form of control: suppression. By the time the gay movement hit the scene, the sexual revolution was over. It had accomplished what was necessary to loosen the grip of a sexual legalism that was based more on coercion than inspiration, more on form than content, more on fear than love.

In the previous chapter, I suggested that simply coming out of the closet as a lesbian or a gay man may invite violent reactions. That coming out is viewed as everything from "selfish" to "revolutionary" suggests an overreaction on the part of those who use such words to describe us. Coming out is an act of vulnerability, not of violence. It amazes me that many Christians who react as if coming out were a violent act do not look at themselves and their strong reactions and wonder, "Why am *I* behaving this way?" rather than "Why is this person behaving this way?"

In his book *People of the Lie: The Hope for Healing Human Evil*, M. Scott Peck characterizes evil largely by an inability to be self-critical.[1] I repeatedly witness this in the church as Christians express violent reactions to gay issues, and yet proclaim they are not homophobic. God knows even *I* am homophobic! How could *they* have escaped it? A straight woman wrote me that she was radicalized on the gay issue by mentioning the subject in a church peacemaking committee, only to have a pastor tell her that if she knew of anyone with a gay son, he "would be happy to beat the [expletive] out of him"! This is a *moral* reaction? That's what such people claim.

Peck's description of various aspects of group evil is chillingly reminiscent of the church's response to homosexuality. Characteristic of that response is inertia, which I've mentioned earlier as a reason for the church's inability to adequately address gay and lesbian concerns. Peck describes it as a group's "lazy unwillingness" to expend energy to change its attitudes. The group "can't even *imagine* itself to be wrong." Related to this is ignorance, which allows the group to depend on "experts" (read here "conservative theologians"), who lead the group into an "unwitting villainy" (read here "ostracism of homosexuals"). Another characteristic response is putting up a "pretense of blamelessness" while destroying evidence that reveals its evil. How many times have I witnessed "blameless" pastors or church bodies destroy gay and lesbian people vocationally and personally, and still somehow believe that they are doing "right"! And then their dirty work is frequently covered up, allegedly for the sake of the individual or the church.

One final characteristic of group evil I will mention from Peck's fuller list is narcissism, which a group may express in several different ways: wanting everyone to be like them (read here "heterosexuals"); creating an enemy "out group" (read here "homosexuals"); and the failing group, potentially the most evil and vicious, which refuses to risk its own brokenness with self-criticism or reevaluation of its positions. Church denominations which are losing members fall in this category, which may explain why they tend to be quick to reject homosexual Christians because the issue might "split the church."

In making our witness, lesbian and gay Christians must follow Jesus' counsel to his disciples to be "wise as serpents and gentle as doves." In coming out within the church, we should not underestimate the terror this strikes in the hearts of those whose faith is as rigid and unyielding as the steeple of the church in the dream described earlier. Nor should we underappreciate the fear this raises in the hearts of those whose faith may not be so rigid, but whose faith is nonetheless based upon the foundation laid by the church of their youth, a church largely unaware and uninformed by the lesbian and gay Christian experience. To challenge rigid faith stances, or scrutinize the foundations of faith, calls into question the whole structure. Of course, this is what the work of the Holy Spirit has always been about, from the days of the early church to its later reformations.

I believe that most gay Christians view ourselves as reformers rather than revolutionaries. The fact that we could not gain the church's attention for much-needed reform before homosexuality became an ordination issue is not our choice. Many churchpersons, some well-meaning, have told me, "You gays made a political mistake, forcing the ordination question first." But that was not our decision. That circumstance was a product of the church bureaucracy, which would not take us seriously *until* we applied to become ministers. But, given this opportunity at reform, we have tried to become "wise as serpents."

Within my own Presbyterian denomination, we ordain not only ministers, but other church leaders as well: elders and deacons. When our national governing body offered "definitive guidance" against ordination of homosexual Christians in 1978, it was interpreted by some church leaders as legally binding on presbyteries (regional governing units which oversee the ordination of ministers) and on congregations (which oversee the election and ordination of elders and deacons). A few congregations balked, however, passing resolutions affirming that they would welcome gays and lesbians into full church membership, with the opportunity of election and ordination to church leadership roles. This served as the nativity of the More Light movement within the Presbyterian Church (U.S.A.). It is a movement which encourages churches to perform acts of *ecclesiastical* disobedience by ordaining gays and lesbians as elders and deacons, much as civil rights activists might perform acts of *civil* disobedience to change unjust laws or to refuse cooperation with unjust systems. The More Light movement, so named because of our belief that "God has yet more light to break forth from God's Word" (Pastor John Robinson's advice to the departing Pilgrims), has led to similar movements in other denominations. The Methodist Church has Reconciling congregations. The United Church of Christ has Open and Affirming congregations. The Lutheran Church has Reconciled in Christ congregations.

Though these movements are small, they are perceived as threatening. One congregation's More Light statement became the subject of an ecclesiastical court case which worked its way up the various levels of the Presbyterian judicial system. At the national level in 1985, our denomination's Permanent Judicial Commission, in a split vote, found the More Light statement to be in error. The church was forced to rewrite its statement.

The following week I had my own dream about the church. I was in a large Presbyterian church, a traditional brick structure, containing a traditionally white, middle- to upper-class congregation, worshiping in a traditionally formal way. And I was angry. I stood up and shouted out my anger. With profound, prophetic insight I spoke spiritual truths and described how they affected political realities within the church. I spoke clearly, precisely. Although angry, my passion was focused and effective.

I woke from the dream, unable to recall the profundities which had come from my lips, unable to remember the spiritual truths or the political realities. All I remembered was anger, the anger of disappointment you feel when someone for whom you hold the highest expectations disappoints you. I felt the anger of disappointment that my church, for which I hold the highest expectations, could once again deny gays and lesbians in this negative ruling from the Permanent Judicial Commission.

But "spiritual people are supposed to be above anger." "Anger only suggests how tied you are to the political realities of this earthly plane." I am certain that some patronizing religious authority said this to Jesus after his rampage in the temple, overturning the tables of the moneychangers and the seats of those who sold pigeons. But Jesus was disappointed. He had the highest hopes for his people, he had passionate hopes for his people. His disappointment was all the greater because his passion for their faith ran so much deeper than theirs. Passion so deep, disappointment so great, produced anger and an angry expression.

Jesus believed in Isaiah's vision for the people of Israel, that they would be "a light to the nations." He quoted Isaiah, "My house shall be called a house of prayer for all peoples," as he removed the clutter of the marketeers from the house of God, the temple of Jerusalem.

The temple was not only the center of Israel's religion; it was the center of their commerce, their politics, and their social life. It would not have seemed unusual for merchants to transact business on temple grounds, especially those Jesus evicted: the moneychangers exchanged Roman coins for temple coins, since foreign currency desecrated the temple; those who sold pigeons provided sacrificial animals for worshipers who did not raise their own animals. So why did Jesus react the way he did?

The clue is Jesus' quote from Isaiah. The quote appears in the following context: "For thus says the Lord, 'To the eunuchs who keep my sabbaths, who choose the things that please me and hold fast my covenant, I will give in my house and within my walls a monument and a name better than sons and daughters; I will give them an everlasting name that shall never be cut off. And the foreigners who join themselves to the Lord, to minister to God, to love the name of the Lord, and to be God's servants, every one who keeps the sabbath, and does not profane it, and holds fast my covenant—these I will bring to my holy mountain, and make them joyful in my house of prayer; their burnt offering and their sacrifices will be accepted on my altar; for my house shall be called a house of prayer for all peoples. Thus says the Lord God, who gathers the outcasts of Israel, I will gather yet others to me besides those already gathered'" (Isa. 56: 4–8).

The temple was divided into three sections. The inner section, the Holy of Holies, which contained the Ark of the

Covenant, could only be entered by the highest of ordained priests once per year. The second section outside the Holy of Holies contained the altar of sacrifice, and only the men of Israel could enter here. The third section, outside the wall of the second section, was the area in which the women of Israel, eunuchs, and foreign converts could draw close to the God of Israel. It was this third, outer section, which Jesus cleared of merchants.

I hope the significance of Jesus' passion to clear this third area is not lost on you, both in terms of powerful concept as well as empowering passion. In angry disappointment that his people could fail to live up to God's call through Isaiah, Jesus cleared the part of the temple in which you and I could stand: as women, as gay men and lesbian women, as Gentiles, as people of color. The gospels of Matthew, Mark, and Luke report a further step in God's revelation in Jesus Christ: at his death on the cross, the curtain separating the Holy of Holies was torn from top to bottom, indicating God's greater accessibility to us all. In life and in death, Jesus turned the temple upside down!

Not only by coming out, but also by speaking out, lesbian and gay Christians are turning the church upside down. Our presence in the church seriously challenges the childhood faith of other Christians. But making our witness is making room for others like and unlike ourselves, even if it means expressing anger in the house of God. We cannot be satisfied as long as lesbian and gay Christians are denied access to that house. We cannot reflect on the great issues of the day if we don't first take up the issue of our own people's oppression. If *we* don't reflect faithfully, theologically, and scripturally on our experience as gay and lesbian Christians together, such reflection is left up to the very people who wish to exclude us. If *we* don't overturn the tables of church bureaucracy as Jesus did, who will make a place for other gay and lesbian Christians to draw near to God?

Cheryl is severely crippled. She has metal braces on her legs, two metal crutches support her arms. Her hands and face are disfigured because she lacks complete muscle control; she speaks haltingly, with a slur, belying the brilliance of her mind. I thought at first that she supported my gay activism because we recognized similarities in our struggles to be accepted as we are and as the ministers we felt called to be. This was true, but it took her nearly a year before she trusted me with the whole truth: she is gay, and as she told me, streams of tears came down her cheeks, her grief inconsolable. "I have enough difficulties in the church without this being known, too," she said. She wants to do theology for the handicapped. But as a *lesbian* woman, who will make the church accessible to her?

At Christian gatherings, Melissa will wink at me from across the room while she continues her earnest conversation about the black experience of God with other black Christians. In a private moment, she'll grab me by the arm and take me aside to find out how things are going. She seldom talks about herself with me; she *has* told me her story, though: she is a lesbian and has a lover, but cannot afford to speak openly about it even with, and perhaps especially with, black comrades. An ordained minister, she believes being both female and black are already two strikes against her in the power structures of the church. "Three strikes and I'd be out!" she tells me, if her church knew her to be a lesbian. But we share her secret across a room of black and white Christians, when her eyes catch mine and we share a smile. Who will defend Melissa's ministry in the church?

Francisco is a church bureaucrat, elevated less by ambition than by his pastoral attributes which make him a kind of "pastor's pastor." Though appreciated by everyone, his kin-ship ties to Latino Christians are particularly strong. Yet he knows their conservative and fundamentalist bent well enough to keep his personal life private, so they know noth-ing of his being gay or of his lover. But this hasn't kept him from being an advocate for gays and lesbians in the church, and it has gotten him into trouble. Some people within the church are trying to get him fired or pressure him to resign because of his support of gay concerns, which puts him through a lot of stress. This, plus the reactionary mood of the church on the whole matter, makes him feel unwelcome: "If they don't want us," he asks, "why stay in the ministry?" Francisco has devoted twenty years of his professional life to the church. Who will applaud and protect such devotion?

Pamela is a respected church educator. She has devoted a lifetime to teaching the gospel to young people, not only administering an expansive church school program in a local congregation, but developing curricula designed for use throughout her denomination. In middle age, she is still con-sidered a desirable and potential marriage partner, frequently introduced to single men and invited out on dates. She doesn't decline these introductions and invitations for fear that her sexuality might be questioned. But she'd rather be spending time with her partner of twenty-five years. And she wishes she could introduce her at church functions as more than a friend. Who will teach the church on *her* behalf?

Sam is the minister of music in a large, evangelical church. His credentials, reputation, and achievements make him a valued and sought-after church musician. Very recently, he tested positive to HIV antibodies. At the same time, the senior pastor has sensed that he is gay and is forcing him to resign from his position. His greatest fear is that if he doesn't leave quietly, the pastor will accuse him publicly, making it virtually impossible for him to find employment elsewhere. His HIV status makes him fear losing both his job and his health coverage. The stress he is now experiencing is detrimental to his health. Who will represent his interests in the church?

Jeff is a longtime church member and a close friend of his pastor's family. At the same time that he finally reconciled his homosexuality with his faith, Jeff was diagnosed with AIDS. The pastor, at first supportive, affirmed his decision to acknowledge his being gay and having AIDS before the entire congregation during worship. Doing so, he received their prayerful support. But this disgruntled some financially influential members, and they brought pressure on the pastoral staff and church council to immediately condemn homosexuality as a sin in a variety of public statements. Now Jeff feels unsupported, rejected, and alienated. Who will bring healing to Jeff?

Christine serves as a volunteer in the Sanctuary movement, aiding undocumented Central American refugees. She worships in a Sanctuary church and has been arrested for the cause. Despite the progressive, even radical Christian milieu in which she gains support for her Sanctuary activities, she does not feel confident enough to come out as a lesbian to her colleagues in the movement. They do not seem to welcome this issue. She wishes that they could offer sanctuary to her as a lesbian woman as readily as they do to strangers. Who will speak up for Christine?

If Jesus were around, he would speak up for all of these. If Jesus were here, he'd clear out a place in the church for them. If Jesus were here, he'd shout angrily, "God's house shall be called a house of prayer for all people."

Of course, the Spirit of Jesus Christ *is* here. So is the Body of Christ. Gay and lesbian Christians are also the Body of Christ. We can speak up for people like these. We can clear a place in the church for them. We can insist that the church be as inclusive as it was meant to be. The tearing of the temple curtain means we do not need ordination as priests to have access to our God.

And Christians will say of us, "Those who have turned the church upside down have come here also."

CHAPTER 14

Opening
Blind Eyes

The "gospel" according to televangelist Jerry Fal-well: acquired immune deficiency syndrome (AIDS) is God's way of "spanking" the gay community. The gospel according to John: "And [Jesus'] disciples asked him, 'Rabbi, who sinned, this man or his parents, that he was born blind?' Jesus answered, 'It was not that this man sinned, or his parents, but that the works of God might be made manifest in him'" (9:2–3). Here Jesus contradicts the age-old notion that phys-ical disability or illness is punishment for the sin either of the suffering individual or of the parents.

Jerry Falwell's response has all the pastoral comfort of one of Job's friends! The book of Job in Jewish scripture addressed the problem of why the good suffer. Job's friends assumed that Job had sinned. Why else, they reasoned, would he lose his property, his family, and his health? Rather than offering a theological rationalization, the story explores Job's faith in the midst of his suffering, while Job's friends kept searching for something in him to blame.

In the midst of the suffering Jesus witnessed, he did not search for blame. He looked for faith in those who suffered, not for sin. The stories of the healings he effected abound with revelations of the faith of those who were healed, as well as of God's powerful love manifest in Jesus' healing touch. The blind man allowed Jesus to put mud made from spit on his eyes, then followed his instructions to wash in the Pool of Siloam, both acts of trust in Jesus. Jesus sometimes pronounced a forgiveness of sin in his healings, but never suggested that those who were disabled or ill were more sinful than other human beings. In this story, he clearly sets aside a primitive association of disability or illness with an individual's sin.

Many Christians, gay and nongay, were therefore rightly dismayed at Falwell's conclusion that AIDS and other diseases are God's way of punishing us. But his conclusion is based on assumptions commonly held by many Christians. Indeed, this issue was debated at a recent General Assembly of my own Presbyterian denomination, a church which prides itself on enlightened views. To challenge Falwell's conclusion, we must critique the underlying assumptions which may distort even our own theology.

No matter how theologically liberated we may believe ourselves to be, in the attic closet of our minds persists the image of God as a punitive force, a punishing parent, or disciplinary father. This is more a god of wrath than of compassion, a god of vengeance rather than mercy. If we step out of line, then we are punished, no matter what Jesus may have explained about God sending rain and sunshine on the just and the unjust, indicating equal divine treatment of us all.

A secular version of this punitive theological imagery is a lingering societal belief that if a person becomes ill or physically disabled, the person must have created the conditions to cause it and is personally responsible. When AIDS was first related to promiscuity and drug-abuse, some in the broader gay community and society at large too smugly judged, "That's what you get for living in the fast lane!" Now that we see that AIDS occurs in gay and straight people who express their sexuality more conventionally, that judgment doesn't hold. Those who consider *all* expressions of homosexuality unconventional may still hold this view, like that of the cartoon (kept out of most newspapers) showing Mother Nature pointing at two emaciated AIDS patients in a hospital bed and saying, "It's not nice to fool Mother Nature." It is true that we are learning how much responsibility we must take for our own health, from colds to cancer and heart disease; but we cannot always control our environment filled with stress, toxic chemicals, radioactive wastes, bacteria, and viruses.

What we *can* do in relation to AIDS is to educate ourselves about safer sexual practices, change any sexual behavior that is dangerous to ourselves or others, avoid drug and alcohol abuse or anything that suppresses immunity or interferes with sound judgment, take care of our bodies with proper rest, exercise, and nutrition, discover if we have been infected with HIV through an antibody test, and, if we test positive, follow the suggestions of a doctor experienced in AIDS treatment. This will include having T-cell counts checked on a regular basis, as well as use of medication to enhance immunity or retard HIV. Changing our sexual expressions may require friends or support groups that will encourage us to overcome the behaviors borne of the permissiveness of the past. We were afforded this permissiveness because we found ourselves outside of conventional sexual mores, often discouraged from forming ongoing relationships, and thus encouraged to engage in anonymous encounters. While disregarding the notion that AIDS is God's punishment, we do need to realize that AIDS makes many previous sexual expressions in which we engaged life-threatening rather than life-giving, thus an evil to be avoided.

Related to the concept that illness is God's judgment is the questionable theological assumption that suffering or calamity is God's way of speaking to us. How many of us have said in the midst of a major disappointment or tragedy, "What is

God trying to say to me?" Or worse, "Why is God doing this to me?" A gay friend who developed cancer on his way to financial success suddenly felt God was trying to shake him up and challenge his values. *Newsweek* reported a young Haitian man with AIDS as saying, "I think God wants me more close to him, that's why he gives me disease."

The problem is, this statement represents an incomplete truth. Yes, we may hear God's voice in the midst of suffering, but we may also hear God's voice in the midst of joy. The blind man heard Jesus' voice in his blindness, but it was after receiving his sight that he could see the Light of the world. Jesus had said to his disciples earlier in the story, "As long as I am in the world, I am the light of the world" (John 9:5). When Jesus asked the formerly blind man if he believed in the "Son of Man," a messianic reference to Jesus, the man asked, "And who is he, sir, that I may believe in him?" Jesus said, "You have seen him, and it is he who speaks to you." The man replied, "Lord, I believe," and the gospel reports that the man then worshiped Jesus (John 9:38). The story suggests that we may recognize Jesus in wellness and well-being as much as in sickness, blindness, and suffering.

Yet history and recent liberation theologies remind us that God is more often the God of the poor, the dispossessed, the oppressed, the imprisoned, the hungry, the homeless, and the disabled. I believe that such people are more likely to search for God than the self-satisfied wealthy, "normal," and well. The latter describes the Pharisees, who objected to Jesus' restoring the blind man's sight on the Sabbath and thereby breaking the law against working on the Sabbath. Like many Christians today, many Pharisees equated success and normalcy and health with God's favor, just as they associated the man's blindness with God's disfavor. The Pharisees could have been instructed by Job's philosophical response to the temptation to "curse God, and die." Job said, "Shall we receive good at the hand of God, and shall we not receive evil?" (Job 2:10). Within good and bad, within agony and ecstasy, we may hear God's voice and see Christ's light.

The Pharisees' self-satisfaction prevented them from looking for God's Word in the prophet Jesus. Just as Jesus proclaimed it almost impossible for the rich to enter the kingdom of heaven, the Pharisees were too satisfied with their religious beliefs and positions to recognize Jesus as the Light of the world. Of them, Jesus concluded, "For judgment I came into this world, that those who do not see may see, and that those who see may become blind" (John 9:39).

Related to the incomplete truth that God speaks through suffering is the notion that God actively *wills* suffering. In Job's story, Satan causes Job's calamities, but God allows Satan the destructive power, which is almost as bad. In the story of the blind man, Jesus' disciples in effect ask if it was God's will that the man was born blind. As God's will unfolds in the story, it is clear rather that it is God's wish for the man to have his sight, because that is precisely what happens. It is also evident that God would rather have the Pharisees open their figuratively blind eyes as well.

Finally, a prevalent theological assumption is that God is all-powerful, an understanding which threatens the belief that God is all-loving, because a God who is both could stop human suffering. This conflict has been discussed in chapter 11. By this understanding, God is believed to be in control of both personal and global destinies.

A church member dealing with a serious illness had finally relaxed her fears and decided that all was in God's hands, when suddenly a minister of our church was wantonly murdered. "What happened to God's controls?" the member wondered. If God were in control, our congregation would have felt forced to conclude that God at worst caused, or at least allowed, the minister's murder. But that seemed preposterous. In this tragedy, our congregation was more willing to affirm God as all-loving than all-powerful. For us, God's loving vulnerability in Jesus on the cross served as a more effective icon than God's almighty invincibility in the history of the Israelites. Jesus on the cross helped us believe that God suffered with the minister in his violent death, and that God suffered with us in our pointless loss. God's power was love in the midst of suffering.

Related to the assumption that God is all-powerful is the belief that God will keep us from suffering if we follow the right formulas. God will take care of us and give us prosperity if we obey God's laws. This was the attitude of Job's friends. This was the underlying belief of the Pharisees who questioned the blind man about his recovery of sight. It is this way of thinking that is reflected in Jerry Falwell's statement.

And shockingly, many gays have flocked to New Age metaphysicians who share a similar attitude. Even more than Christianity, these teachers would have their followers believe that if they adopt the right attitudes and actions, they can prevent illness, prolong life, and prosper vocationally and economically. Clearly, there is spiritual wisdom in these teachings. I do believe that a prayer of affirmation brings more healing than a prayer of confession usually does, partly because I believe that positive reinforcement is a more effective means of transformation than negative training. But the liability of such a belief system is that people who become ill or die feel responsible and guilty for their condition. At the same time, it fails to take into account the spiritual reality that people who do what is right may suffer, and indeed may suffer precisely because they are doing that which is good. In the case of AIDS, some persons with AIDS (PWAs) are suffering because they have *loved* someone who happened to be infected. Because of this, it is difficult for me to understand why those who are "wounded" by HIV infection (or any venereal disease, for that matter) in the process of *love*making are treated less respectfully than soldiers who are wounded in the process of *war*making!

Jerry Falwell concludes that AIDS and other diseases are God's way of spanking us. He arrives at this conclusion by means of assumptions, commonly held by Christians and the broader society, which must be questioned: God is a punishing parent; suffering people deserve to suffer; suffering is God's way of speaking to us; God wills us to suffer; God is all-powerful; suffering indicates God's disfavor; God will stop our suffering if we do what is right. These assumptions could lead to the ludicrous conclusion that the crucifixion was God's way of "spanking" Jesus Christ!

Jesus himself tried to lead us from these misunderstandings of God's nature. He illustrated God as the forgiving father who welcomes the prodigal home. Jesus modeled God's compassion by wanting to gather the suffering "like a mother hen gathers her brood." Jesus communicated God's will not through coercion, but by persuasion through parables, teachings, and self-sacrificing love. Jesus Christ did what was right, and yet he was called to suffer more than most to fulfill his ministry.

Ironically, when Jesus healed the blind man, he exposed the spiritual blindness of the self-righteous Pharisees. Blinded by their law, they resented Jesus healing on the Sabbath and thereby breaking the rules. Blinded by outdated theological assumptions, they believed the man was born blind as God's punishment of sin. Blinded by their self-righteous pride, they believed the formerly blind man "born in utter sin" could not instruct them. Blinded by religious or professional jealousy, they believed Jesus himself was a sinner. Blinded by their arrogance, they believed they could see God's will better than anyone else. "Some of the Pharisees near [Jesus] said to him, 'Are we also blind?' Jesus said to them, 'If you were blind, you would have no guilt; but now that you say, 'We see,' your guilt remains'" (John 9:40–41).

And the irony of our story as gay and lesbian Christians opening our blind eyes to our self-worth is that our healing reveals the spiritual blindness of modern-day self-righteous Pharisees. Blinded by their laws, their outdated theological assumptions, their self-righteous pride, their religious and professional jealousy, their arrogance, they cannot see that Jesus has touched us and called us.

Spiritually blind, the Pharisees refused to listen to the blind man's testimony of Jesus' healing miracle. Ultimately, they rejected Jesus himself. So modern-day Pharisees refuse to listen to our testimony of Jesus' restoration of our self-esteem as gays and lesbians. They want to find blame in us, our parents, or even the fall of Adam and Eve, for our homosexuality.

"Rabbi, who sinned, this one or the parents, that this person was born homosexual?"

"It was not that this one sinned, nor the parents, but that the works of God may be made manifest."

Opening blind eyes reveals the deeper blindness of the Pharisees. Then *and* now.

CHAPTER 15

Manifesting
Christ's Glory

The whole of the New Testament testifies that God's divine glory was manifest in the birth, ministry, and resurrection of Jesus Christ. The whole of church tradition and history testifies how imperfectly Christ's divine glory was manifest in those who followed him through the centuries. But there have been times when the Spirit moved over the chaos of the church and called forth great lights to reform it. Lesbian and gay Christians are yet one more light revealing new dimensions of Christ's glory.

Anticipating a Messiah hundreds of years before Christ's birth, the prophet Isaiah wrote, "The people who walked in darkness have seen a great light" (Isa. 9:2). Almost a hundred years after Christ's birth, John wrote, "And the Word became flesh and dwelt among us, full of grace and truth; we have beheld Christ's glory, glory as of the only Child from God" (John 1:14).

Expectation and retrospection perhaps come easier than insight into the present moment. Both the light and the glory of Jesus' nativity were obscured by the realities of the situation. Joseph and Mary had contracted to marry. Unwed, Mary became pregnant, and Joseph sought to divorce her privately to avoid scandal. But Joseph's dream and Mary's vision revealed the nativity would be of the Holy Spirit.

In the Jewish council of the Sanhedrin, the pragmatic religious leader Gamaliel would later say of the nativity of Christianity: "If this movement is merely human, it will die of its own accord. But if it is of God, you will not be able to stop it, and you might find yourselves opposing God" (Acts 5:38–39). Jesus' nativity was a movement of the Holy Spirit. The child was to be called Emmanuel, which means "God with us." Movements of the Holy Spirit mean that God is with us. In them, we behold God's glory.

The dictionary defines "nativity" as birth, especially with reference to place, time, and accompanying conditions. There are many nativities conceived of the Holy Spirit whose place, time, and accompanying conditions have been described either in scripture or tradition. Prophets anticipated or recognized them, and the community of faith realized God at work, often in retrospect. Pentecost was the nativity of the church. The inclusion of Gentiles into the previously exclusive Jewish sect of Christianity served as the nativity of the church's global mission. The Reformation of the sixteenth century became the nativity of Protestantism and a revitalized Roman Catholicism. In these and other movements of the Holy Spirit, we have beheld Christ's glory.

The Spirit is not barren. Even today, she gives birth to movements in the church and in the society, nativities of which it may be said, "If this movement is merely human, it will die of its own accord. But if it is of God, you will not be able to stop it, and you might find yourselves opposing God." Perceiving God at work, prophets cry, "The people who walked in darkness have seen a great light." And, looking back, the people of faith later rejoice, "We have beheld Christ's glory."

But at the time of the nativity, both light and glory are obscured by the realities of place, time, and accompanying conditions: the awkwardness, the scandal, the simplicity, the humble origins—all of which mysteriously belie the miraculous aspect of nativities of the Spirit. Yet these births also proclaim that God is with us. Jewish scriptures used the birth metaphor for the inbreaking messianic kingdom. In describing the catastrophic events leading to the fulfillment of time, Jesus himself used the term "birthpangs" in Matthew 24. And in Romans 8, the apostle Paul viewed all of creation—as well as all people of faith—groaning in an ongoing birth process.

The birth of the present gay movement is also a nativity of the Spirit. In the gloom of heterosexism and homophobia, prophets have proclaimed "More light!" Future Christians will rejoice in the movement's nativity, confessing, "We have beheld Christ's glory." In the meantime, both light and glory are obscured for the majority of Christians. Isn't that the way with any of the Spirit's movements? There are always distant leaders like Caesar Augustus who haven't the slightest idea what's happening in their realms. There are fearful political or religious leaders, Herods and Sanhedrins, who are afraid that what's happening might challenge their power and control. And there are inhospitable innkeepers who have no room and strangers who fail to recognize the Spirit at work.

Thanks be to God that, when the Spirit gives birth, there are also always the poor, who, like the shepherds, welcome the interruption of God's messengers in their lives. And the wise, who, like the Magi, find themselves outside the immediate experience but have insight and perspective to understand the significance of the event. There are silent partners like Joseph, who support and sustain without requiring public attention for themselves. And those like Mary, who risk the scandal of impurity to labor in the pain and anguish of childbirth.

The lesbian and gay movement has also coped with distant, ignorant, and fearful leaders in government, society, and religious institutions. We have negotiated with those who have no room for us, whether in employment, accommodations, health care, or worship. We have told our stories to strangers in hopes that they might understand.

Again, thanks be to God, there have been the figuratively poor who have viewed us as God's messengers: closeted gays and lesbians, as well as our parents, spouses, children, and friends eager to understand. There have been wise scholars who have shed light on our contributions to church and society, as well as illumined the sociological and historical reasons for our mistreatment and our present emergence. There have been silent partners who have quietly offered expertise and finances to support and sustain gay and lesbian organizations within religion and society. And there have been those on the forefront of our movement who have risked life, livelihood, and reputation to give it birth.

In this birth of the Spirit, Christians will be blessed if they behave more like shepherds than Sanhedrins, more like wise ones than innkeepers, more like Josephs than detached strangers. In the nativity of the gay movement, the church might well heed Gamaliel's counsel, "If this movement is of God, you will not be able to stop it, and you might find yourselves opposing God."

I believe that faithful Christians eventually will not prove distant, ignorant, nor fearful of our cause as gay and lesbian Christians. Preachers will make room for us in their sermons and services, and parishioners will make room for us in their pews and pulpits. Strangers will come to know us as Christians whose worth is recognized and whose gifts are welcomed. People who walked in darkness about the lesbian experience and the gay male experience will see more light. And the church of the future will reflect on the presence of the Holy Spirit in the nativity of the gay movement within Christianity by confessing, "We have beheld Christ's glory."

It was not only in Christ's nativity that God's glory was manifest. God's glory was also revealed in his life and ministry. Similarly, Christ's glory must not only be manifest in our nativity as a gay movement, but also in our life and ministry. "Nobody knows the trouble I've seen," moans the old black spiritual. And it wasn't until blacks made their troubles known that things began to change for them. Gays and lesbians have pursued a similar strategy, not only coming out of the closet ourselves but bringing our troubles with us. Airing wounds brings healing, no doubt, but how many people want to see somebody's scabby wound?

And sharing our troubles is often like throwing pearls before swine. I've heard heart-wrenching stories of lesbians and gays to which other people have responded that we "brought it on ourselves" by "choosing perversion," and that we were "injustice-gathering individuals." Human potential movements have a nicer way of saying it: "You created that experience." Yes and no. I may choose to be vulnerable by saying who I am, but I do not choose to be hurt.

Regardless of our right or need to speak of our grievances, we must consider their effect. During a retreat for a social justice committee that was intended to energize and inspire us, a process consultant pointed out that we had debilitated ourselves by rehearsing the failure of church policies to effectively change society. Attending a national gathering of lesbian and gay Christians, I experienced the same enervating negativity, both in personal stories and in reflections upon church inaction on gay issues.

I have done my share of reciting personal and ecclesiastical tragedies. Speaking in a church in upstate New York, I was shocked by the "heaviness" of my own presentation. I intuited the audience needed to hear a call to repentance implied by gay sorrows because their hearts were so hardened against us. This speech contrasted sharply with an upbeat talk I gave in another church in the same city that week. There I sensed that the sympathetic audience was all too aware of gay troubles and needed to hear of God's commonwealth reflected in gay hope. I believe different people may need to hear different stories. Certainly Jesus himself was harsher with those who refused to listen, while gentler with those who tried to understand.

Black women and men making known their troubles wasn't and isn't enough to change hearts. It may have cracked open some white people's armored hearts, much like people crack their doors to hand out a donation to a charitable organization soliciting on their doorstep. But it didn't necessarily make anyone eager to invite them in. It is as blacks and whites experience one another in a fuller way that a mutual welcome is possible.

Consider your own experience. Do you look forward to the visit of a positive, multi-faceted friend with a sense of humor, while dreading the visit of a negative, single-issue person who takes everything too seriously? We all have our days of hopeless, single-focus seriousness. But we as lesbian women and gay men realize we don't simply want a handout from the cracked door of others' hearts: we want to be welcomed inside. We don't want to be patronized or matronized. Even the unrepentant homophobe can pity a person with AIDS, giving us the opportunity of literally being patronized *to death!* We are realizing that we don't want the sympathy of those who are not gay; we want their interest.

That "nobody knows the trouble [we've] seen" is true. But it is also true that too few people know the *glory* we have also seen. Being dispossessed in the church has offered us a unique opportunity to rely on God and God's grace, feeling more keenly God's embrace than those who already feel accepted. If nobody else loves us, God's love becomes all the more dear and precious. Being "outlaws," outside conventional mores that keep heterosexuals in line, we have learned the value of inner direction over external control and have been given opportunities to experience more nuances of love and lovemaking.

of us who are Christian have had to rely more heav-
ile Spirit's guidance than on that of the church. Re-
rom the millstone of the institutional church, our
spirits have soared in creativity and compassion and celebration. And many of us have gained a thirst for justice and
liberation for all who are excluded. We join black churches
in teaching mainstream churches about inclusiveness, passion
for justice, and the joy of praising God!

Jesus said, "Let your light so shine before others, that they
may see your good works and give glory to your Creator who
is in heaven" (Matt. 5:16). And Paul wrote the church at
Corinth: "Therefore, having this ministry by the mercy of
God, we do not lose heart. . . . For it is the God who said,
'Let light shine out of darkness,' who has shone in our hearts
to give the light. . . . We are afflicted in every way, but not
crushed; perplexed, but not driven to despair; persecuted, but
not forsaken; struck down, but not destroyed; always carrying
in the body the death of Jesus, so that the life of Jesus may
also be manifested in our bodies" (2 Cor. 4:1, 6, 8–10). I've
already written much about our identification with Jesus'
death on the cross. Now I write about what it means for the
life of Jesus to be manifested in our bodies. I believe that
from our chrysalis-closet birth to our prophetic vision of the
church as chrysalis-tomb, we serve as witnesses to resurrec-
tions yet possible.

God's glory was manifest in Jesus' resurrection, as well as
in Jesus' nativity and ministry. Though Jesus' resurrection is
central to Christian faith, it is a big stumbling block for many
Christians and would-be Christians. Christians believe in the
living presence of Jesus Christ in our world today, but, affirming the resurrection of Jesus Christ forces some of us to confess with the father who sought healing from Jesus for his
epileptic child, "I believe; help my unbelief."

One of my college professors recounted his experience
seeking ordination before a church committee determined to

discover if he shared their understanding of the resurrection. "Tell me this," one queried, "if you were present at the tomb on that first Easter morning with a Polaroid camera, would you have been able to take a picture of Jesus coming out of the tomb?" The professor thought a moment, then replied, "Yes, but only if the camera were equipped with the lens of faith!"

As Christians, we stumble over the resurrection when we confuse a confession of faith for a statement of historical fact. It is when we treat matters of faith as matter-of-fact that we miss the mystery, the meaning, and the extraordinariness of our faith. Peter pointed out that only people of faith were given sight of the resurrected Jesus: "God raised him on the third day and made him manifest; not to all the people but to us who were chosen by God as witnesses" (Acts 10:40–41).

From the first Easter, Christians have held different views on the nature of the resurrection. All of the earliest gospels, Matthew, Mark, and Luke, suggest a bodily resurrection. But the latest written gospel, that of John, suggests a spiritual resurrection: Mary Magdalene, Peter, and John discovered the linen cloths which wrapped the body still in place, ex-actly as they would have been if the body were still there. This is clearer in the Greek text than in English translations. The author of the gospel of John apparently believed that Jesus' body was transformed spiritually, hence leaving his shroud in place. Otherwise the cloths would have been strewn on the floor of the burial cave or at least laid aside.

Several resurrection stories in the other gospels confirm this physical transcendence, reporting Jesus' request not to be held, his appearance through locked doors, and his disap-pearance after breaking bread. Others confirm Jesus' bodily presence as he eats with the disciples or encourages Thomas to touch the wounds in his hands and his side. The latter story combines physical presence and mystical vision, for though the disciples are able to touch their Savior, he appears in their midst through locked doors. With all these variant descriptions of the resurrection, it's safe to say Jesus' first followers were not nailed down to a bodily interpretation. If the early Christians were not of one mind as to the nature of Jesus' resurrection, why should Christians today require such uniformity of belief? I believe the resurrection would be less a cause for doubt if a diversity of opinion were welcomed.

However interpreted, both the Incarnation and the Resurrection are among our most precious theological affirmations. The Incarnation, expressed in the story of the nativity, is the affirmation that, in Jesus Christ, God has entered and become part of our world in human form. The Resurrection, told in the context of the crucifixion, is the affirmation that God has vindicated Jesus and his gospel by giving him victory over sin and death.

Regardless of their views of the resurrection, the early Christians soon realized that they themselves would have to incarnate Jesus Christ in the world. The intense experience of Jesus' presence among them faded, and this was explained by Jesus' ascension into the heavens. Now the church would serve, as Paul articulates in his letters, as the Body of Christ in the world.

Certainly the early disciples incarnated Jesus' resurrection in their sudden turnabout from defeated followers of a leader who died a disreputable death to the victorious ambassadors of Christ who founded a movement which would change the course of Western history. No historical fact alone can explain this conversion. Only the confession of faith that "Jesus Christ is risen" could have turned their depression and despair into joy and hope. The subsequent gift of the Holy Spirit at Pentecost empowered them to boldly embody the resurrection. Jesus had told them this Spirit would lead them to further truth and enable them to do greater things than he himself was able to do. The nativities of the Spirit described earlier attest to this as the church sought to be inclusive, to reform itself, and to manifest Christ's glory to the world.

To me, nothing seems further removed from manifesting Christ's glory than being forced to discuss the scriptures quoted against homosexuality. One year, during the Lenten season in which Christians prepare for Easter, a chapter of Dignity (the Catholic organization for gays and their supporters) invited me to make such a presentation. Frankly, I did not want to talk about those same tired old scriptures once again. But I dusted off my notes, and did so anyway. Many of those in attendance were parents, college roommates, or friends of gays and lesbians. What I had to say was received warmly and positively.

During my drive home, I thought about what I would say to my congregation on Easter Sunday. I wondered what the resurrection means to the present generation, as well as within the gay and lesbian context. In a community which witnesses so many crucifixions, how can we open eyes of faith to resurrection? Then I remembered the gathering which I had just left. I considered the gratitude of lesbian and gay Christians and the gratitude of those who loved them dearly for the liberating words I offered about the liberating Word. I witnessed new life within them and within me. And it dawned on me, "*This* is the resurrection!"

I realized the role of all gay Christian ministries, and specifically that of the Lazarus Project of the West Hollywood Presbyterian Church: our ministry was manifesting the resurrection of Jesus Christ in our bodies. When we shared Christ's Communion with gay inmates of the Los Angeles County Jail, sacramentally assuring them that one may be gay and Christian, for them *we served as the resurrection.* When we saw the face of a gay teenager light up with hope as he listened to gay Christians from our speaker's bureau, we realized, *we served as the resurrection.* When a lesbian in a small town in Maryland wrote to say she thanked God every day that our church existed, we recognized that, for her, *we served as the resurrection.* When one of us in a bar on a Saturday night met someone who believed no church would welcome him until he was invited to our church, we knew *we served as the resurrection.* When we celebrated the love of two women or two men in a Christian ceremony and saw their tears of joy, we celebrated that *we served as the resurrection.* When someone feeling suffocated, lonely, and alienated came into our sanctuary to breathe in the free and fresh air of communion, love, and support, we could believe that *we served as the resurrection.*

It's time to get off our crosses and manifest the resurrected life of the Body of Christ. As that Body, we manifest Christ's glory in our nativity as a gay and lesbian Christian movement. As that Body, we manifest Christ's glory in our life and ministry as lesbian and gay Christians. As that Body, we manifest Christ's glory by serving as the resurrection for others. By manifesting Christ's glory, God's glory is revealed to the world.

"We have beheld Christ's glory." "So that the life of Jesus may also be manifested in our bodies." "Jesus Christ is risen today!" Hopefully, within us. "Lord, we believe; help our unbelief!"

CHAPTER 16

Evangelizing

If you experienced a negative, visceral reaction to the title of this chapter, it is because many evangelists and evangelicals have given this word a bad reputation. In a previous chapter, I described a gay church member who made a remarkable transformation from being unable to say the words "Jesus Christ" to being enabled to declare him Lord of his life. But he could never bring himself to use the term *evangelism* because of its negative connotations for him, though he himself served as an evangelist in our jail ministry. Indeed, it was difficult to keep him in a committee meeting if the word were mentioned!

Evangelism comes from a Greek word in the New Testament which means "good news." An evangelist was one who brought good news. The word *angel* comes from this word also. Angels traditionally were bearers of good news: "glad tidings" in the case of those who announced Jesus' birth to the shepherds. So it is ironic that the words *evangelism, evangelist,* and *evangelicals* have come to mean "bad news" to many of us.

There are several reasons for this. Those of us who grew up in evangelical traditions became aware that evangelism was too often reduced to gaining new members for the church, rather than bringing good news to people in need of it. Too often, the emphasis was on attracting attractive, talented, and successful people rather than others who might benefit more from hearing of God's love. On the other hand, evangelism programs which were less concerned with church membership often offered good news in word but not in deed. That is, the good news became a verbal and "spiritual" communication rather than one which included any earthly help, such as food, clothing, shelter, counseling, or advocacy.

Near my church I once passed a pushy street evangelist pressing an obviously cornered street person to "accept Jesus as Lord and Savior" so that he wouldn't "burn in hell". This is the crassest form of evangelism: one that treats salvation as a type of desperately needed business transaction.

Not far behind in tastelessness is the "Hollywoodization" of evangelism which came with the televangelists. Local radio and television preachers in the past and the present have well served the homebound—those for whom church attendance has been prohibited by illness, disability, or distance (such as in rural areas). But the glamorization of slick evangelical celebrities has led to unbridled egos, outrageous scandals, distorted faith, and a television audience isolated from one another and detached from a sense of community. They have made bad biblical scholarship, popular psychology, and conservative to reactionary politics palatable to an unknowing public by special effects, palatial set designs, friendly banter, and dramatic oratory.

Evangelical Christians themselves are often viewed as rigid, conservative, and moralizing, as biblical literalists, and as aggressive in their attempts to convert individuals and society to their way of thinking. The recent collaboration of evangelical Christianity with the far political right further heightens suspicion of evangelicals, especially for gays and lesbians whose freedoms are among the targets of the religious right.

Last year I attended the funeral of Edith Allen Perry, mother to the founder of the Metropolitan Community Church and a saint in the cause of lesbian and gay Christians. In the sermon, Rev. Nancy Wilson repeated a funny remark that she had once made about her son, Rev. Troy Perry. "I'm glad Troy turned out to be gay," Mrs. Perry had said. "Why?" Nancy had asked, surprised. "Because when he was in the Pentecostal church, he was a good preacher, a good evangelist," Mrs. Perry said, "but he was very narrow-minded. Being gay opened him up to all kinds of things!"

With frequent associations of narrow-mindedness, no wonder evangelism carries so many negative connotations! But I believe that we need to reclaim the words *evangelism*, *evangelist*, and *evangelical*. A dozen years ago, during a meeting of the Presbyterian Task Force to Study Homosexuality, Professor George Edwards from Louisville Presbyterian Theological Seminary described himself as a "liberal evangelical." He explained that he did not want to abandon a perfectly good, prophetically Christian word to legalistic, moralistic conservatives. He believed that his concern for social justice, his advocacy for the oppressed, and his liberationist biblical scholarship were all as much or more good news than what those who traditionally termed themselves evangelical offered.

Also owning or reclaiming the word are many gay and lesbian evangelicals. The nationwide organization Evangelicals Concerned coalesces these with nongay evangelicals who are supportive of gay concerns. Throughout the country, chapters of this group meet for prayer, Bible study, and fellowship.

Other countries refer to all Protestant churches as "evangelical." With a small group of Methodists and Presbyterians, I visited Nicaragua in 1984. Our host was Nicaragua's national council of evangelical (Protestant) churches. It was quite a contrast from the anti-Sandinista sentiment among American evangelicals to discover that Nicaraguan evangelicals supported their new government!

I believe that lesbian and gay Christians should not only reclaim the word *evangelical,* but acknowledge that making our witness has been an evangelical activity. We are bringing good news to lesbians and gays of God's love in Jesus Christ. We are bringing good news to Christians that sexual orientation is not a criterion for admission into the commonwealth of God. We are bringing good news to families broken by the church's condemnation of gay family members. We are bringing good news to congregations torn between the gifts of lesbian and gay parishioners and the demands of denominational policies on homosexuality. We are bringing good news to the gay community, witnessing our integration of spirituality and sexuality as well as the integrity of spirituality and social justice activity. We are bringing good news to all Christians, demonstrating that sexuality may be affirmed and enjoyed in the context of spirituality.

Working with a largely gay congregation for ten years, I found that the most difficult witness we made was with our own gay brothers and lesbian sisters. Making witness to the broader church was tough, but making witness to another gay person was both tough and intimate. Sharing one's faith is frequently a more intimate activity than sharing one's sexuality. For some of us, being sexual with someone came more easily than being spiritual with someone. In preparation for a gay pride march in which we planned to participate, a church committee debated the production of tee shirts with our church's name on them. I suggested that "West Hollywood Presbyterian Church" be emblazoned on the back of the shirts in big, bold lettering. But the committee chose instead a discrete logo on one side of the front of the shirt, with the church's name in tiny lettering. Though church members might have been willing to wear tee shirts with their favorite beer or radio station writ large on them, they didn't want their favorite church's name or logo to be too obvious. I would have thought they'd be proud to wear the church's name, as well as happy to share the good news of our inclusive congregation with others through this seemingly non-threatening means.

Lesbian and gay Christians have learned the liability of sharing the good news of our faith, however. Just as sharing our sexuality within the church has allowed many Christians to dump on us all their negative feelings about sexuality, so sharing our faith within a gay context has allowed many gays and lesbians to dump on us all their negative feelings about religion. Sometimes all their anger at the church seems directed to us. Sometimes they become as moralistic as church folk, demanding, "How can you say that you're Christian and gay?" Sometimes their unresolved conflicts between faith and sexuality inspire ambivalence toward us in friendships and relationships. Sometimes a disheartening indifference is expressed, and we feel pained that something of importance to us is considered boring to them. And sometimes they are so passionately interested in reclaiming their spirituality that we can't change the subject!

Bob Patenaude, an active church member, enjoys telling a story illustrating the latter. Having been reared as a Presbyterian, he proved extremely interested when he overheard me tell someone in a bar that I worked at a Presbyterian church. He kept asking me questions about it until I finally reached in my pocket, pulled out a church business card, and, handing it to him, politely excused myself with the words, "Come to church sometime and we can talk more about all this."

No matter which response one receives when affirming one's faith, it can be emotionally draining. I must confess that there are times when I am with gay people that I avoid mentioning my life's interest as a method of self-preservation!

Yet I do feel called to share the good news and the community of faith that empowers and inspires me.

On a personal retreat at Mount Calvary Retreat House in Santa Barbara, I devoted my reading time to Reformed theology, that is, theology which grew out of the Protestant Reformation in the sixteenth century. Though aware that my own thinking was influenced by Reformed perspectives, I felt I lacked a comprehensive understanding of this theological foundation.

Among my fellow guests at the retreat house were two young gay men, a couple, who had come for their own retreat of a few days. In a dinner conversation with them and a priest of the order, I learned something about them. One was Roman Catholic, and the other called himself Protestant, though unaware of his particular denomination. The Catholic spoke in the language of New Age spirituality. The Protestant didn't seem to have any religious language with which to speak. Both were there to develop their spirituality and to "find themselves," but, they made it clear, without the interference of organized religion. My typically liberal reaction and that of the priest was to commend them for their efforts without questioning their anti-religious stance. "Few things are necessary for the spiritual life," the priest affirmed. But, I thought to myself, this priest is saying this after thirty years in the order and in the priesthood! Surely this is a conclusion that most appropriately comes toward the end of spiritual development rather than at its beginning. One can't offer a spiritual pearl like that without opening a lot of oysters!

As I observed these young men, separated even from each other, trying to "free-lance" their spirituality in the gardens and the natural surroundings of the retreat center, I began to feel very sad. They did not seek counsel from the brothers in the order. They did not speak with me about being a gay Christian. They did not attend the prayer services, so they did not hear scriptures, sermons, stories of saints, nor receive the sacrament of the Eucharist. They were cut off from several millennia of spiritual experience and tradition as well as from a spiritual community which transcends time and death.

They probably would not act this way in any other area of their lives. If they developed their bodies, they would go to a gym, listen to training tips, and learn what they could about health and nutrition. If they wanted to do maintenance and repair on their cars, they wouldn't go by "feelings." If they took up painting, they would probably learn the technology of their craft as well as take an interest in the history of art.

It occurred to me that true revolutionaries know the tradition against which they are rebelling. Radicals go back to "roots," from which the very word *radical* comes. And, as I read of the Reformers and read the Reformers' own words, it was apparent that true reformers can ignore neither tradition nor community. The Reformers' critique of the church of their day grew out of two communal experiences of faith: that represented in scripture, and that represented in the church of their day. And scripture offered them their traditional foundations.

True, these gay men were not intending to be revolutionaries, radicals, or reformers. They wanted to feel good, improve themselves, and discover inner peace. These are probably the primary motivations of all who cultivate a spiritual life. But the Reformers reacted against such goals as the sole motivations of the religious. Thomas Aquinas had written, "Man's ultimate felicity consists only in the contemplation of God." Over against this celebration of a vision of the perfection of God, John Calvin set the vision of God's kingdom, a vision which calls us to action within God's will. In his book *Introduction to the Reformed Tradition,* John H. Leith writes, "The glory of God and God's purpose in the world are more important than the salvation of one's own soul. Personal salvation can be a very selfish act. . . . Human beings are religious, the Calvinist asserts, not to satisfy their needs or to give meaning to their lives, but because God has created them and called them to service."[1]

During the same trip to the Holy Land in which I experienced Christ's spirit ministering to my need for feelings of well-being and peace on the Sea of Galilee, I had one other vivid experience of Christ's presence. But it did not offer me peace. I visited Yad Vashem, the memorial to those who died in the *Shoah*, a Hebrew word for annihilation, a term sometimes preferred to the redemptive implications of *Holocaust* as a free offering to God. The building is designed to look like a giant block crushing skulls, rounded stones taken from the shores of the Dead Sea. The entrance is a wrought-iron interpretation of barbed wire. On the floor of its darkened interior are simply the names of the Nazi death camps, with an eternal flame burning. The horror and the grief so simply and starkly represented immediately moved me to tears. Christ's passion for justice flashed through me as a righteous flame demanding action to prevent such evil from ever happening again. Years later, a similar experience awaited me as I viewed panels of the AIDS quilt memorializing victims of AIDS when I visited the offices of The Names Project in San Francisco. Such experiences call me to move beyond merely dealing with my personal concerns and to hear God's call to serve others.

During my visit to Mount Calvary Retreat House I experienced a call to share the good news of my spiritual tradition and community with these two gay men. My sadness grew from knowing that offering to do so would be met with the same indifference, arrogance, or judgmentalism I might meet with by making a pass at someone who had not invited such intimacy. Two other young men, on the road to Emmaus, recognized the Christ in their midst because they listened to a fellow traveler expound the scriptures and welcomed him into their communion, sharing sanctuary, bread, and wine.

There are others in the lesbian and gay community who *would* welcome our faith, our spiritual tradition, and our Christian community. Our faith is based in the good news that God loves us in Jesus Christ. Our tradition speaks of a God who acts and calls us to action within God's broader purpose. And our community of lesbian and gay Christians and those who support us may provide other sisters and brothers a much-needed spiritual home.

A woman with a drug problem told me how much she envied my belief in God. Wistfully she described her friends in Alcoholics Anonymous and Overeaters Anonymous, and how their belief in a Higher Power helped them to overcome their addictions. "If only I could believe in something like that," she sighed, "maybe I could get off drugs."

One Christmas, our church distributed invitations for our Christmas Eve dinner to all the young male prostitutes working along Santa Monica Boulevard in West Hollywood. Perhaps we too clearly established that our intent was not to force God or religion on them. Rather plaintively, one asked me, "If we *want* to talk about God, that's okay, too, isn't it?"

A lesbian whom I met at a party wanted to remain Christian, but all the imagery about God as male and as father in her tradition made her believe it was a man's religion. Unaware of the current community of Christian feminist writers, she asked me, "How can I embrace Christianity as a woman?"

A friend who has tested positive to HIV antibodies periodically asks me questions about my faith, about God, about

Jesus. He wishes that, at death, some emissary from God would tell him exactly what to believe. But, until then, we who are lesbian and gay Christians may be the only ambassadors from God that he will trust.

The good news, the evangel, of which we make witness to lesbian sisters and gay brothers is: they do not have to *find* themselves alone. They do not have to find themselves *alone*. God rushes out to greet them, welcoming them home, embracing them with the two arms of tradition and community. And that loving hug can inspire and empower all of us to live out God's will, contributing to God's broader purpose of the salvation of the world.

As evangelists, having been entrusted with this gospel, let's preach it. "As for you," the apostle Paul wrote young Timothy, "always be steady, endure suffering, do the work of an evangelist, fulfill your ministry" (2 Tim. 4:5).

PART V

Declaring Our Vision

As the epistle to the Ephesians describes the reconciliation of Jewish and Gentile Christians, so might it describe the reconciliation of straight and gay Christians: "For Christ is our peace, who has made us both one, and has broken down the dividing wall of hostility, by abolishing in his flesh the law of commandments and ordinances, that he might create in himself one new person in place of the two, so making peace, and might reconcile us both to God in one body through the cross, thereby bringing the hostility to an end" (Eph. 2:14–16).

"There is one body and one Spirit, just as you were called to the one hope that belongs to your call, one Sovereign, one faith, one baptism, one God, Mother and Father of us all, who is above all and through all and in all" (Eph. 4:4–6).

The vision that we bring to the church and the church to the world is that peacemaking is *making the world safe for diversity* (chapter 17). Gay and lesbian Christians bring a new understanding of *healing*, which we define as integrity rather than uniformity (chapter 18). We lead the church in *healing AIDS*, healing persons with AIDS, the "worried well," and those who love and care for them (chapter 19). Ultimately, "what we did for love" is what God remembers as God graciously welcomes us home, where we enjoy *loving eternally* (chapter 20).

Making the World
Safe for Diversity

When I lived alone, I sometimes felt the need to
be with people, even if they were strangers and the association was seemingly impersonal. Occasionally I treated myself
to breakfast, coffee, and people at the local McDonald's. If
you've never noticed, our morning meal gets its name because eating it means we break our overnight fast. Most obviously, breakfast at McDonald's broke my fast from food.
Less obviously but more importantly, it broke my fast from
people. This unconventional communion had the essential
ingredients of every communion: children of God.

Thomas Merton, the Roman Catholic contemplative, once
wrote that his solitary retreats enabled him to return to people and see them with a new vibrancy, as if witnessing their
glory as God's children for the first time. Returning from a
personal retreat of my own, I breakfasted at McDonald's and
discovered what Merton meant. Beginning with Dana, the
young black "priest" who smilingly administered the sacrament of the Egg McMuffin, to the nameless "deacon," a
Spanish-speaking "alien" whose eagerness to clear my table
had to be warded off when I went to the counter for a refill
on coffee, I witnessed a procession of people with whom I
shared something deeper than my faith: a fragile humanness.

The communion I celebrated required eyes of faith, of course. As is true in much of life, most of the partakers were too busy with their own thoughts, conversations, newspapers, books, food, or plans for the day.

A nervous, grey-haired man jolted past me as if getting an additional napkin were the most crucial act of his existence. When he returned to his table, I noticed he was reading the same newspaper article I had been reading—a study which reported that 60 percent of Americans surveyed declared themselves to be happy. As he read, he rocked from side to side; the short cigar in his mouth rolling in the opposite direction, as if it were a counterweight.

Nearby, two young women spoke too loudly. They seemed to be in a kind of daze that one might associate with drug abuse. "Go see if my breakfast is ready," one commanded. The other woman obediently brought her meal. "Did you get me a game chance?" the first woman asked plaintively, referring to McDonald's Diamond Hunt game. "Yes," came the resigned reply. Taking her chance the first woman exclaimed, "Wow! Now I've got eighteen chances." She spoke of what she'd do "when" she won.

A carefully dressed businesswoman and her young son sat down in the booth next to the nervous man with the cigar. The boy stood on the seat, turned toward the man, pointed to the cigar, and asked, "What's that?" The man's lips twitched excitedly into a smile as he replied, "Now that's a cigar." The mother instructed her son to turn around, eat, and stop "pestering" the man. The man returned to reading about happiness.

Across from the teenage women, two young men were engaged in an earnest conversation. One was exceptionally attractive, dressed in a smart silver jacket. The other bent his head down and began to cry softly, trying to avoid public attention. His curly haired friend—his lover, I supposed— watched him caringly. He looked around, as if searching for help. If only I wore a clerical collar, I thought, they'd know I was available for help. Then it occurred to me that someone in clerical clothes would probably be the last person to whom they'd turn.

The nervous man stood to leave, smiling and waving good-bye to the little boy who was still fascinated by the cigar. The young woman rich in chances to win diamonds suddenly decided to give half of her chances to her friend. The silver-jacketed young man reached out a comforting hand to his crying friend, fondly grasping his forearm and then his hand.

I felt awed by the scene. The commonwealth of God had come near, spontaneously forming community. The vision was friendly and homey. Of course, I was looking for the friendly and the homey. I had been alone on my retreat. And most of my life had been spent in the lonely retreat of a closet. I was looking for community, for communion, for home. I believe my search is not uncommon among others who have spent years in the closet. I also believe that the lonely place of the closet makes many of us value other people with an unusual intensity.

Years ago, the journalist Heywood Broun described walking down a New York City street with a professional explorer. Suddenly the explorer said, "I hear a cricket chirping." Broun didn't believe that his friend could hear such a small thing in the din of city traffic, until his friend pushed aside some litter at the edge of the sidewalk to reveal a cricket. Then the explorer took a coin from his pocket and dropped it on the same sidewalk. Several people heard it hit the sidewalk and stopped to look for it. The explorer told Broun, "People see what they're looking for, and hear what they're listening for."

Having experienced a comparatively happy home life in my youth, both with my biological family and my church family, I looked for a similar experience as an adult with a lover, with gay family, and with a church family that would welcome me home. My activism on behalf of civil rights, peacemaking, and, later, gay rights, grew from a desire to enlarge my experience of home, a place "where they have to take you in," regardless of race, nationality, or sexual orientation.

Because I was looking for it, I was able to perceive relationship among strangers at McDonald's. But sometimes life experiences interfere with such vision. We are tempted to say that "reality" dampens our inspiration, but I believe that the vision is as much reality as what actually takes place. The writer Charles Williams believed that "disillusionment" in a relationship is a misnomer, because it is based on the assumption that one's original vision of a person was an illusion. He went so far as to suggest one's first vision of a lover may be the truer reality. I can only affirm that a vision may be at least as real. Therefore, to discard a vision may be as unrealistic as to discard what happens in life.

While embracing the reality of the approaching Holocaust during World War II, a young Jewish woman named Etty Hillesum proclaimed her vision of what life was intended to be in her diaries, recently published in English as *An Interrupted Life*. As the Nazis were transporting the Jews of Holland to detention centers and death camps, Hillesum searched for the good in humankind and the makings of home wherever she went. Trying to understand what in a Gestapo officer's background or present life might cause him to mistreat her, she concluded, "What needs eradicating is the evil of man, not man himself." She also wrote, "I am with the hungry, with the ill-treated and the dying, every day, but I am also with the jasmine and with that piece of sky beyond my window." Weeks later, wondering what to pack should she be transported, she observed, "There will always be a small patch of sky above, and there will always be enough space to fold two hands in prayer." And reflecting on a visit to the Westerbork camp, she wrote, "I have no nostalgia left, I feel at home. I have learned so much about it here. We *are* 'at home.' Under the sky. In every place on earth, if only we carry everything within us.'"¹

In reference to my ability to adjust to new places, I have often said that "Home is where the heart is, and my heart travels with me." And though that's true, there was one time when I left a part of my heart and lost a home. It was a time when reality, in nearly obscuring a vision, actually revealed it.

Weary from a month's trip through India, I eagerly looked forward to returning home. I longed for my lover's arms. But he wasn't at the airport to meet me as planned. Later I learned that he was in Hawaii with someone who would become his next lover! I was devastated. We had made plans to spend our lives together; his home had become mine. Now I had no home. I returned to my own apartment, but it didn't feel like home. I experienced the most intense grief of my life. I had met with disappointment in relationships before, so I wondered why this one proved so overwhelming. I knew I'd recover, but I wanted to know why my feelings ran so deep. I sought the help of a therapist whom I trusted, an ordained minister who, though not gay, had also been hurt by the church. Gradually, it became clear in my healing process that I had lost more than a partner in life; I had lost *home.*

My vision of home had been a motivating factor in my life's ministry: trying to make the broader church a welcoming environment for lesbians and gays, as well as creating a comfortable sanctuary for lesbians and gays in a local congregation. I learned that, because of the demands of the role I played, the broader church and the local church could not quite serve as home for me. The one home I had grown to depend on was the safe haven my lover and I had created together. Now I had lost that sanctuary.

In such desolation, it is not comforting to hear Jesus' description of his own ministry: "Foxes have holes, and birds of the air have nests, but the Human One has nowhere to lay his head" (Matt. 8:20). These words tell us that Jesus understood this yearning for home, but they do not assure the earthly fulfillment of such a hope. Yet, in the story of the final judgment, Christ rewards his followers who provided a home, saying, "I was a stranger and you welcomed me." Perhaps it is in making a home for another that we find a home for ourselves. It was a vision of homemaking that enabled me to get beyond my temporary setback and discover someone with whom I have finally found home.

I believe that the vision of homemaking keeps many lesbian and gay Christians in ministry within the church and within their community. Christian scholar John Boswell shares that vision. During one of his visits to Los Angeles, he gave a lecture on those periods in church history when homosexuality was tolerated and sometimes celebrated. At a clergy luncheon a minister asked what were some of the special graces gay people had to offer the church. The first grace that Boswell mentioned was our ability to treat one another as family. "If one of us needs someone to talk to, someone to turn to, or a place to stay," he said, "it's my experience that gay people more readily welcome one another as if family. This is a less common experience in the nongay community." He added that there is also much more cross-cultural, cross-ethnic, cross-economic, and cross-vocational blending in our relationships, friendships, and extended family formations. We have created home for one another in the midst of a society and church which treats us as strangers. And that has been one of our saving graces throughout history.

After the luncheon, I drove Boswell to my favorite place to walk, a place which has been home to me from college days: the palisades overlooking the shore in Santa Monica. When I have needed to reflect on life, I have found it helpful to seek out a place like the seashore, where God's natural graces abound. I have often walked along the pathway in the park on the cliffs, and then along the beach beneath. That day was particularly beautiful as Boswell and I walked and talked, occasionally pausing to appreciate the Southern California coastline.

Down on the beach, we came to its gay section. I hardly needed to point it out to John, as he had already sensed the presence of gay family. As we turned toward our ascent back up the palisades, we walked through the pedestrian tunnel that runs beneath the Pacific Coast Highway at this point. I told John of a graffiti writer who, a few years earlier, expressed his objection to the gay beach by writing "Faggots, go home!" many times along the walls of the tunnel. The gay response was to paint the word HOME! in big letters on a wall at the beach end of the tunnel. In other words, this gay beach *was* our home.

One of our special graces as lesbians and gays is that, in the midst of unwelcoming environments, we have created homes. Like Etty Hillesum, we have realized that "We *are* 'at home' . . . in every place on earth, if only we carry everything within us." Our vision has given birth to gay neighborhoods, to extended families inclusive of gay, bisexual, and straight persons, to the nesting of couples.

For everyone, the world is a transient and rootless place, as people move to follow opportunities of career, housing, education, culture, and relationships. Our traditional expressions of family are changing for a variety of sociological reasons. There are millions of single adults, and the potential for isolation and alienation grows. As Jesus made his home with the family of faith, so the church in these circumstances may serve as a home for people regardless of marital status, sexual orientation, single parenthood, or nonmarital sexual expression. Instead of forcing everyone to adhere to a single definition of family, the church could welcome everyone into the family of faith. In the often unwelcoming environments of our world, I believe that gay and lesbian Christians could help make the church safe for such diversity.

The church is called to be in the world as well. Too much of governmental domestic and foreign policy is based on the presumption of uniformity of experience, belief, and practice among the peoples of our nation and among the peoples of the world. Every nation could learn from a God who chooses to lead the world toward peace through persuasion rather than coercion. Instead of remaking the world in our own image or depersonalizing those who are different in condition or outlook, we could welcome one another in the home God has provided for us all.

Making the world safe for diversity—perhaps that is ultimately our call: to be peacemakers. Maybe peacemaking is, at heart, nothing more nor nothing less than homemaking, creating a church and world which *has* to take everyone in, which *wants* to take us all in: fragile, human, strangers, who also happen to be children of God.

CHAPTER 18

Healing

Planners of a churchwide educational event in Texas invited me to colead a workshop on homosexuality and the church. The other workshop leader was to be a person who had begun a "healing ministry" for homosexual persons. He was bringing a "healed" homosexual man to participate in the workshop, so I taped an interview with a black church member who had experienced another so-called healing ministry, and I used portions of the tape in the class. The workshop participants heard of the sexual exploitation and spiritual domination this individual endured at the hands of such ministry. It was only when he began worshiping with our congregation and attending the Lazarus Project Bible study group that he enjoyed true healing.

But those attending the workshop could have learned the bogus nature of ministries which claim to change homosexuals by listening carefully to the prime example of the healing ministry showcased by my co-leader. The supposedly "healed" homosexual revealed that the ministry's counseling worked by having the clients develop a deep emotional attachment to their same-gender counselors. This satisfied their need for such a relationship while denying them an opportunity for sexual expression. In response to a question, the healed homosexual surprised many when he confessed that he still had homosexual fantasies. He described as an example passing a

183

jogger in his car and mentally undressing him. Then he gave
a detailed description of what he would enjoy doing with the
runner's genitals, a description I would blush to record here!
I thought to myself, "Here *I* am the professing gay person,
and though I may admire a male jogger, I don't get into such
an elaborate fantasy!"

His fantasy life was apparently compensating for his loss of
real-life experience. Jesus condemned those who judge sins of
the body when the judges themselves indulged in sins of the
mind: "every one who looks at a woman lustfully has already
committed adultery with her in his heart" (Matt. 5:28). And
to think that the relationship that the healed homosexual
had with his counselor was intended to serve as a substitute
for a truly loving relationship—such "counseling" violates
good ethics and good sense! It would make the client dependent on the therapist, when good psychotherapy seeks to help
the client realize his or her independence.

In the workshop, I presented another alternative. I re-
claimed the words "healed" and "healing" by offering myself
as an example of a healed homosexual leading a ministry that
was healing to other homosexual persons as well as healing
for the church. In my own healing process, accepting my
homosexuality within the context of my Christian faith led
me to a reconciliation with God, with myself, with my family
and friends, and with my church. The Spirit enabled me to
integrate my spirituality and my sexuality, to give thanks to
God for both, and to praise God for God's wonderful deeds
in liberating me from my own homophobia and the homophobia of others. My worship became more holistic, my gratitude more authentic, and my ministry an outgrowth of what
God had done for me. I then sought to reconcile externally
what the Holy Spirit had reconciled internally: homosexuality and Christianity.

When Jesus healed, he removed obstacles that prevented
the worship of God. The cleansed lepers could return to their
worshiping community by showing the priests that they were

no longer infectious outcasts. The woman healed of a hemorrhage by touching his garment would no longer be considered "unclean" by the strict religious code. The demoniac could worship Jesus when the demons which crazed him were sent into a herd of pigs. The hungry multitudes could better listen to Jesus' words after he healed their hunger by feeding them.

Jesus healed more than met the eye. When he healed the beloved servant of a Roman centurion, Jesus acknowledged the faith of a Gentile, and someone who represented the oppressor. "Not even in all of Israel," Jesus exclaimed, "have I found such faith." When he allowed the woman of ill-repute to wash his feet, over the objection of the Pharisee with whom he was dining, he welcomed her into intimate communion with himself and healed her of her estrangement from the community of faith. Healing was not the arbitrary restoration of a person's abilities or health, it was the removal of that which interfered with an individual's worship of God. In these latter two stories, the healing overcame questions of condition and morality, and welcomed the Roman and the woman into spiritual community and communion.

Lesbian and gay Christians have experienced this kind of healing within our own lives. Our affirmation of this healing is often perceived as an affront to the church, I believe, because of its own failure to adequately reconcile sexuality and spirituality. Regardless of their viewpoint on whether or not homosexual persons are "broken" and in need of "healing," many Christians hold the view that homosexuality is an issue wounding the church, causing brokenness. What they fail to see is that homophobia and heterosexism are what is truly wounding the church, and that the church, in turn, is wounding its gay family members and neighbors and encouraging society at large to do so.

A recent General Assembly of the Presbyterian Church, meeting in St. Louis, approved guidelines for its own exhibit hall, an area set aside for church agencies and organizations to display their programs and ministries. In a list of things which would not be tolerated in exhibits, a list which included things like racism and sexism, this national governing body voted not to include homophobia, though previous assemblies have declared it to be a sin. Just after the vote, a gay seminarian sat down near me. Hurt by the assembly's action, he said, "I just can't believe they wouldn't include homophobia in that list. I guess it's okay to hurl abuse at gay people."

That very night, as I walked a gay Pentecostal to his car after a two-hour counseling and prayer session, a car of drunken young men careened toward us, hurling abusive language attached to the word *faggots*. Our goodbye hug must have seemed suspicious to them. On their third pass, they drove as if they intended to run us down. My friend, nervously trying to catch his breath, urged me to get into his car. He drove me the short block back to my hotel.

Ironically, one of the arguments that our opponents use is that church opinions should not be "dictated" by society, as if our society embraces gays and lesbians! That night, in the General Assembly vote and in these abusive men, I personally witnessed how the church and society become conspirators in their dysfunctional relationship with homosexual persons.

The incident with the gay-bashers reminded me of a similar experience one Sunday as members of my congregation enjoyed coffee hour after worship. Another group of young men drove past those of us standing outside the sanctuary and, instead of hurling the usual anti-gay epithets, simply shouted one word: "AIDS!"

The same evening that the General Assembly refused to include homophobia in its guidelines, it debated a fairly enlightened policy statement on AIDS. But the assembly removed an affirmation that AIDS should not be viewed "as punishment for behavior deemed immoral." In effect, they declined to take issue with the judgment that AIDS is God's judgment on homosexuality. From a gay perspective, it was difficult for me to discern a difference between the church's position and that of those who drove past our church shouting, "AIDS!"

Gay Christians are seeking to bring healing to the church, to restore its "peace, unity, and purity" by restoring gays and lesbians to the church and by restoring the church to gays and lesbians. The healing of our sexuality and spirituality may lead to the healing of the sexuality and spirituality of our heterosexual counterparts in the church. Our healing presence may lead the church to a more inclusive prayer life, a more inclusive ministry, and a more inclusive community. We are evangelicals in the radical sense of the term. We are bearers of good news.

I believe lesbian and gay Christians are living reminders of the healing that Jesus offered persons of faith. The goal of this healing is integrity rather than uniformity. "Your faith has made you whole," Jesus told the woman healed of the hemorrhage, not "Your faith has made you like everybody else." The healings effected, the demons cast out, enabled those who benefited to return to their homes, neighborhoods, and synagogues. Families, communities, and congregations were made more whole by the reintegration of those who had been exiled. Both individuals and groups enjoyed greater integrity, greater wholeness.

I define integrity as an integration within the self of what one believes, thinks, says, is, feels, and does, accompanied by an integration of that self with community, creation, and Creator. Created in God's image, human beings reflect God's ability at integration, though not God's capacity. Lacking trust in God, we reach for God's capacity in the prideful belief that we may do so and play God's role. This is illustrated by Adam and Eve's eating the forbidden fruit of the tree of the knowledge of good and evil to "become like gods."

Another biblical example is the building of the tower of Babel, a human attempt to reach into the heavens. In trespassing on God's turf, we "dis-integrate" ourselves from harmony with God, with creation, and with our community. Biblically, such harmony is represented in the past by Eden, and in the future by the kingdom, or commonwealth, of God.

The Law of Moses became a means of reintegration, harmonizing the self with the community, and the community with God. The Law was the people's side of the Covenant between God and the people of Israel, indicating the mutuality of the brokenness. When the Law became perceived as a new Tower of Babel, that is, a human attempt to reach into God's heaven, Jesus Christ was called to reintegrate us with God and the cosmos. The Church was charged with this ministry of reconciliation: to reintegrate the self, and the self with God, creation, and community, by putting us within the healing touch of Jesus Christ.

I define brokenness as denying our interior wholeness and denying our integrity with the Creator, creation, and community. The story of creation tells us that we are made in the image of God. Jesus' healing touch proclaims "the kingdom of heaven is within you" and "your faith has made you whole." The Fall was not a fall from perfection, but a fall from integrity—a "dis-integration." Adam and Eve did not trust their integrity with God, with one another, with all of creation. They believed that the knowledge of good and evil would lead to their perfection, to their becoming "as the gods."

People of faith throughout the centuries have supposed that knowing and doing good would lead to their perfection, to their becoming godly. The perfectionist ideal unprovidentially led to debilitating anxiety ("If I can't become a saint like Mother Teresa, I won't pray regularly!") or undue pride ("I'm on the road to perfection while these slobs are whiling away their lives!"). In present-time America, I believe this has led to the opposite experiences of low self-esteem and the unquestioned self. I believe that most Americans suffer from low self-esteem, unable to affirm their integrity as people made in the image of God. Christian admonitions against pride are rendered meaningless and even destructive in the face of this sense of worthlessness. Those who need to hear it the most cannot: the unquestioned selves, those who are too sure of themselves, their answers, and their god.

I define healing as affirming our wholeness and affirming our integrity. Healing implies "returning to its original state." Our original state is wholeness and integrity, having been made in God's image. *Therapy,* derived from the New Testament Greek term for healing, is the process of returning to our original state of wholeness. Healing means change, and change may be painful or discomforting. But healing is engineered into the process of life: a cut hand heals, certain blood cells fight foreign bodies to prevent infection. So, our brokenness may be healed, whether of flesh from flesh or flesh from spirit. God's Spirit leads us to affirm our wholeness and integrity, heals disintegration, even (as our faith affirms) the ultimate disintegration of death.

Many Christians mistakenly believe that the healing of our integrity leads to uniformity. I believe that the healing of our integrity leads to unity. Unity respects the integrity of an individual or group, while harmonizing such within a broader scheme. Uniformity disregards the integrity of the individual or group in favor of normality as defined by selective biblical criteria or majority practice. Unity enables broader levels of harmonizing, so that, for example, religion and science are not viewed as opposing forces, but complementary endeavors. Uniformity disables such harmonizing, setting religion against science. Christians who view uniformity as the goal of healing want sexual minorities to conform to heterosexual lifestyles. These Christians cannot accept the findings of science regarding homosexuality and bisexuality, because science is also perceived as the opposition. Christians who view unity as the goal of healing may be more tolerant of sexual diversity, believing that unity may lead to shared experience and insights. These Christians more readily accept scientific information related to sexuality.

The liability of Christians seeking uniformity is that they are readily seduced into believing that sexual orientation may be changed, or that directing homosexually oriented persons into celibacy or heterosexual expression will not carry severe psychological, emotional, and spiritual penalties. The liability of Christians seeking unity is that they are readily seduced into seeking unity at all costs, even if it means ignoring or suppressing diversity within the church.

These two kinds of Christians—those seeking uniformity and those seeking unity—are not always separate groups: the boundaries between them are sometimes quite fluid. A Christian may seek uniformity on one issue, while seeking unity on another. Gay and lesbian Christians, in the process of integrating our sexuality and spirituality, most likely find ourselves seeking unity, but that does not necessarily mean that we do not experience or express uniformity of belief and practice.

I believe that Jesus Christ himself opted for unity over uniformity. Class, condition, morality, or theology did not determine to whom he brought the gospel, or whom he chose to heal, or whom he called to serve. He looked for a person's faith in God as healer when he restored people to their integrity, to their community, to their God. In his final prayer for his disciples and all "those who believe in me through their word," Jesus did not pray for uniformity of belief, but for unity, "that they may be one even as we are one, I in them and thou in me, that they may become perfectly one, so that the world may know that thou has sent me and hast loved them even as thou hast loved me" (John 17:22–23).

The goal of becoming "perfectly one," as either church or individual, is not perfection, but integrity. Our healing as a church or as a community is found in our unity more than our uniformity. Our healing as individuals is found in our faith in Jesus Christ, not the Babel tower of a heterosexual law.

CHAPTER 19

Healing
AIDS

"Come home, ye who are weary, come home! Earnestly, tenderly, Jesus is calling, calling, 'O sinner, come home!'"

A friend who served as a church camp counselor told a story of a teenager who fell from the watertower of the camp. The counselors gathered around a phone in the office, waiting to hear word from the distant hospital of the youth's condition. They already knew the only two possibilities: the boy would either die or be paralyzed from the neck down. Grieved, despairing, one woman poignantly sighed, "This is one of those times you wish Mommy could kiss it and make it all better."

Jesus told the story of a teenager who opted for an early inheritance plan and spent half the family resources frivolously. Grieved, despairing, the father waited for his return and recognized his son when he was yet far down the road. Over the objections of the older brother, the father joyously restored the son to the family, surrounding him with the love and riches of home.

Hymn writer Will Thompson cast Jesus as this forgiving father: "Patient and loving, he's waiting and watching, watching for you and for me. Come home . . ."

One night I had a nightmare. I dreamed I had AIDS. Grieved, despairing, I wished it were not so. I wanted to be comforted, for someone to make it all better. I wanted to find home. I woke and realized that I *was* home, home with my lover. I did not have AIDS.

Others in the gay community have had similar nightmares about contracting AIDS. And some have been unable to wake from their nightmare, because they *have* been diagnosed with AIDS. Both groups need the healing resources of *home*. Both need Mom to kiss it and make it better. Both need a nonjudgmental Dad who eagerly waits to welcome them home.

God's providence has given me a supportive and loving mother and father to whom I may yet go in the crises of my life. And though I no longer expect them to find solutions to those crises, I may anticipate their care for me and their care for the one with whom I share my life. Most stress tests give favorable points for having loving family nearby.

But many who are lesbian and gay do not have access to mothers and fathers. Perhaps rejection alienates them. Maybe a move to a more accepting urban area geographically separates them. A closet door may still disable the intimacy required for any true support. One or both parents might be dead. Or relations with parents may never have developed to a place where "home" as a caring environment was anything more than an ideal concept.

Jesus placed the family of faith ahead of the biological family. "Who are my mother and brothers and sisters?" Jesus asked rhetorically, "whoever does the will of God" (Mark 3:33–35). The family of faith is Jesus' family. In his own crisis, the cross, Jesus created a new family relationship. To his mother, Mary, he said of his disciple John, "Woman, behold thy son." And to John he said, "Behold your mother" (John 19:26–27). Jesus knew they would need one another to care for and to be cared by. In coping with the crucifixion, they needed the spiritual home that Jesus created from the cross.

Jesus did not create a spiritual home just for Mary and John. He created a home for us as well, for in his life and death he was bringing us home to God and to one another as his sisters and brothers. For those without family and for those with family, the church may become our spiritual home.

One Lenten season, my lover and I used as a source of meditation a collection of writings from Christians past and present, gathered by Hans-Ruedi Weber in the book *On a Friday Noon*.[1] Each day we took turns reading a text. One morning, as George read Saint Bridget of Sweden's vivid vision of Jesus' suffering on the cross, I had an amazing feeling of recognition. "It sounds like she's describing a person in the final stages of AIDS," I commented. I wondered aloud about what in her own experience could have contributed to her vision. George said, "She lived during the time of the Plague." I was struck with how Jesus on the cross united our experience of suffering across centuries. It was as if Jesus, from the cross, were saying to us of Saint Bridget, "Behold your spiritual mother." Our spiritual home extended across time.

Jealous of Jesus' eagerness to welcome gays and lesbians to their spiritual home, the institutional church has played the resentful, elder brother, refusing to participate in the celebrative feast. The institutional church rejects our reclamation of our Christian spirituality and of our spiritual family as self-affirming lesbians and gay men. In doing so, it also makes the mistake of rejecting our spiritual gifts and insights.

AIDS challenges the homophobia and heterosexism of the church that leads to this rejection. I believe that God is testing the church to see if it will be faithful to Christ's Spirit in meaningful ministry to the leper of the twentieth century. At a Canadian-United States ecumenical AIDS consultation in Toronto, the dominant view of the sexuality discussion section was that the church should refrain from making any more negative statements about homosexuality. As one gay churchman put it, "It's time for the church to pray for the gift of ears rather than the gift of tongues."

In preparation for preaching on Pentecost Sunday one year, I enjoyed reading once again the story of Pentecost, the undoing of the confusion of Babel. God confused the tongues of the citizens of Babel who arrogantly attempted to build a tower to reach into heaven. But in the Pentecost reversal, the Holy Spirit empowers those who would build Christ's church to speak in the tongues of strangers.

Outlining my sermon, I was interrupted by a phone call from a friend with AIDS. "I'm just calling to tell you that I'm ready to let go," he said. I was stunned into silence. For Larry Patchen, this statement meant more than his readiness to die, though that would have been enough. For Larry, a "take charge" personality, this was a statement of faith as he trusted his lover, his friends, his church, and his God to care for him.

Grateful that Larry would call to share this significant sign of spiritual growth with me, I couldn't find adequate words to respond. I looked down at my Pentecost sermon in progress, and wished the Spirit could give *me* a few meaningful words in this moment. Involuntarily, my eyes jumped across the room to a stack of sermons I had been filing earlier that day, sermons which surely had once spoken comfort and courage and challenge to my congregation, and specifically to my friend Larry. But now, as he awaited my response on the phone, they seemed to me no more than my personal Tower of Babel.

Other than eventually stumbling out some expressions of awe and gratitude, the Spirit gave me no words with which to appropriately receive a revelation so valuable. I later realized Christ's Spirit had nonetheless given me a response: silence, a respectful silence, a holy silence, a welcoming silence, a silence in which I could hear my friend's agony at his suffering and my friend's triumph in its conclusion. My friend's faith offered me a sense of peace and calm, alleviating my fears of widespread dying in our community, as well as fears of my own death. His trust in God increased my own faith.

"The church needs to pray for the gift of ears rather than the gift of tongues."

During the Toronto consultation in which I heard these words, I stayed with Henri Nouwen at the l'Arche community called Daybreak in nearby Richmond Hill. L'Arche is a worldwide religious community begun in France by Jean Vanier. It provides home and family for mentally handicapped and often physically disabled persons. Assistants, who come from the ecumenical community, volunteer for extended periods of time to be members of these households. They both assist the disabled as needed and learn from the disabled. As I made my daily trek from Daybreak to the AIDS consultation in downtown Toronto, I realized that the model of healing l'Arche offers might well be used in ministry with persons with AIDS. Healing is understood in its biblical context of restoration to God's covenant community, the household of faith. And healing is recognized as mutual and reciprocal: the ones who may appear most in need of healing also heal those around them.

In describing the consultation to Henri, I told him of my admiration of the persons with AIDS in attendance. Those I met seemed in their manner and ministry to be expressions of God's grace. I expressed doubt to Henri that I could minister in that way. I have felt so vulnerable in the church being open about my sexuality, that I did not wish to add vulnerability to vulnerability. Should I develop AIDS, I thought, I would want to keep it a private affair.

Henri understood. Yet he pointed out that the Christian, as a minister, is a person for others, making his or her death a form of ministry as much as his or her life. Those who surround you in your dying need comforting only you may offer, he explained. Those who embrace you in death need your spiritual insights in facing their own eventual transformation.

Within weeks of my trip, these truths became incarnate, embodied in the death of another friend from AIDS. Lyle Loder had come to the West Hollywood Presbyterian Church years before, becoming an active volunteer. In the congregation he met other former Methodists who decided to reclaim their roots in Methodism and form a chapter of Affirmation. Much to their regret and ours, it also meant leaving our congregation to join one that was United Methodist. But they, and especially Lyle, always expressed gratitude for the environment of our church which enabled them to find one another.

Lyle became the minister he had always wanted to be, though not ordained. The negative stance on homosexuality of his denomination had thwarted his hope long before; now his ministry with Affirmation would challenge that artificial barrier. From his speaking to church groups to conducting the memorial service of his lover, I witnessed firsthand what the United Methodist Church had missed in not affirming his ministry. His diagnosis of AIDS became for him another opportunity for ministry, as he urged the church to become involved in the crisis. A week after returning home exhausted from a Methodist consultation on AIDS in San Francisco, at which he had made an outstanding speech, he was hospitalized for the last time.

At the hospital, a crowd of his friends gathered in the corridor and a small waiting room next to his room. A close circle of friends maintained the vigil around his bed as he lost and regained consciousness. Someone reported to me that, during one of his periods of consciousness he asked them to "tell Chris Glaser that . . . ," but the message was incoherent. I felt honored and humbled that he would think

of me in his final hours. I felt that he had given me a very
special gift.

After an evening commitment, my lover joined me in returning to the hospital. Friends had gone home. Through the
open door, I saw an orderly cleaning Lyle's room. Behind
him lay Lyle's body, still in the bed. The orderly kindly offered us some moments alone in the room. Lyle's face was
uncovered; rose petals had been neatly placed in a cross on
the bedding covering his slight frame. Seeing him and taking
his hand in mine comforted me enormously. Later I learned
that the crowd of friends had eventually been let in one by
one to say good-bye. Having accomplished these farewells,
Lyle died within minutes.

That Lyle comforted his friends in his dying and comforted me even in death, suggests a spirituality gracious and giving, the like of which we rarely see. Lyle Loder had led us
all beside the still waters of death and somehow restored
our souls. The one who seemed in need of healing had
healed us.

Rev. Steve Pieters, a friend who was diagnosed with AIDS
in 1984 after more than a year of bad health, is alive and
well, in remission from both Kaposi's sarcoma and lym-
phoma, and leading a nationwide ministry on AIDS for the
Universal Fellowship of Metropolitan Community Churches.
He attributes his good health to his spirituality, his faith community, the love of his friends, as well as an experimental
drug treatment program. But there was a time, just before his
diagnosis, when he felt abandoned by his church. "The
concept of a young, healthy man getting sick and being
housebound for months somehow didn't register" with his
congregation. "I knew my friends loved me," Steve explained
to me, "but they didn't know how to express their love. They
didn't know if they were up to it, or had the skills for it."

In an interview for a magazine article, I asked him how he
was able to forgive and return to the church. He responded:

"What helped me was what helped me when I came out as gay: a chapter on disillusionment from Dietrich Bonhoeffer's book, *Life Together*.[2] He writes that God's grace acts in disillusionment. God's grace appears when our 'wish dream' of what community should be is shattered. I asked myself if I believed in community, if I believed in the church, and if I did, what did I believe about forgiveness? What did I believe about the fact that my church did not live up to my expectations of community? I remembered all the times I got so angry at people in my parish, when I was pastoring a church, who would respond to disappointment in the community by walking away, going home if things didn't go their way. Remembering that, I thought I'd give my church another chance, and I walked back in. I found that as I practiced forgiveness, I experienced forgiveness." Mutual forgiveness, I believe, is a hallmark of the home experience.

Steve knew that the AIDS crisis would escalate, and that the church needed to learn how to minister to the needs surrounding an epidemic of such magnitude. Finding people in his congregation responsive, together they repaired the cracks in their ministry. Steve's ministry now takes him around the country, sensitizing other churches to the pastoral and spiritual needs of persons with AIDS.

Confirming Steve's own experience, I've witnessed others whose access to genuinely supportive church family seems to enhance their resistance to AIDS. The church could become a home, a source of healing, if it avoided another dreary pronouncement on homosexuality and instead joined Christ in announcing, "Ye who are weary, come home!"

Churches throughout the nation are holding an increasing number of "healing services" for persons with AIDS. I am glad for that, as long as we are not misled as to what healing means within our tradition. Every worship service is to be a healing event, bringing us home to God and to one another. Healing is a restoration to God's community of faith, the removal of any obstacle to that restoration. Therefore, the church must confess and repent of its homophobia and heterosexism. Only then may gays and lesbians, HIV-infected or not, find in the church the healing balm of home. For persons with AIDS, healing may express itself in remission, but it may also mean simply that persons with AIDS will be able to die "at home": at home with God, at home with their family of faith.

A deeply spiritual person once commented, "Given the severe spiritual and emotional stress the gay community has experienced as it comes out in a hostile society, it's no wonder that we would be vulnerable to such a catastrophic illness as AIDS." In our vulnerability, I believe it is the Spirit of God who has moved, called, and empowered our community to be the ministers to our brothers with AIDS that the church has failed to be. In doing so, many of us have learned more from them about spirituality and God's grace than the church was able to teach us. Now, in returning home, reclaiming our spiritual family, those of us who are Christian have much to offer the church in spiritual and ministerial experience.

During one Holy Week, I found myself immersed in grief at the widespread experience of death in our community. A close friend infected with HIV and searching for spiritual hope commented on a 1989 *Newsweek* survey, "If half the clergy doesn't believe there's an afterlife, why should we?"

My pastor's sermon on Easter Sunday was the kind of sermon I would have given, the kind that I have given in the past. Humorously confessing a desire to avoid both heresy and controversy, she chose not to discuss whether there was a physical or spiritual resurrection of Jesus. Instead, she focused on the question put to Mary Magdalene as she wept in the garden of his tomb. Jesus asked her, "Woman, why are you weeping? Whom do you seek?" Mary's grief blinded her at first to the vision of a living Christ. I recognized the connection with my present grief that was blinding me to a living God who is "God of the living." Jesus had argued against the Sadducees in favor of the resurrection of the dead by reminding them that God was called the God of Abraham, Isaac, and Jacob, thus implying their ongoing life, since "God is not the God of the dead, but of the living; for all live to God" (Luke 20:38).

Though my pastor's Easter sermon was excellent, provocative, and comforting, it did not make me celebrative that day. Who was my friend infected with HIV looking for, and whom did I seek? Someone who would tell us that God loved us, loved us eternally, gave us life eternal. My lover and I walked along the cliffs and beach of Santa Monica that afternoon. Santa Ana winds had cleared the sky, and the air was cold and crisp, the sea blue and choppy. But, unlike previous walks in this flood of God's natural grace, the beauty did not heal my troubled soul.

At the end of our walk, we entered a bar named the S.S. Friendship to get some warming coffee. This had once been the gay writer Christopher Isherwood's neighborhood hangout. Sitting down, I looked across the room at a vaguely familiar face. "John?" I said, just as he asked, "Chris?" We had not seen each other for over five years. Typically, on seeing an old friend in our community, I thanked God to find him still alive. George and I invited him and his friend to join us. He seemed relaxed and content, and I was happy to discover that he had been with a lover for five years with whom he had bought a home. With so much death in our neighborhood, I enjoyed finding him well and happy and in a relationship.

He shared his spiritual journey. He reminded me that he had begun as a Catholic. I remembered that he had been a Lutheran shortly before joining the Presbyterian Church. Now he told us that most recently he'd been attending the Church of Religious Science. "I got something I needed in each church, without getting involved in the garbage of each denomination," he admitted. I envied, admired, and resented his ability to avoid the garbage, myself feeling buried in the Presbyterian refuse of committee meetings, petty bickering, and outrageous injustice toward gays and lesbians.

As I asked him about his lover, he said simply, "He died last week." "AIDS?" I asked, astounded that even this idyllic picture could be shattered. "Yes," he said. "He was diagnosed two years ago, and he used what time he had left to help others. It was wonderful to see. We had a good time together. I have no regrets. He died in my arms. I felt him leave his body. That's why I'm sure I'll see him again."

As we later took our leave and I hugged John goodbye, I whispered in his ear, "Thank you for giving me the Easter message I needed to hear today." I had somehow heard the gospel in a gay bar. Just as Mary had been called by name and thereby recognized the risen Christ, so I had been called by name and thereby witnessed a resurrection. Perhaps one of our callings as lesbian and gay Christians is to restore the Easter hope to a church that frequently echoes the skepticism of Thomas. And it will understand Jesus' words to him, "Happy are those who have not seen and yet believed" (John 20:29).

Let us pray that those in the gay community who have felt the need to leave the church may find the welcome of Jesus in the midst of the AIDS crisis. Let us pray that the elder brother, the broader church, may heed Jesus in coming in to our "welcome home" feast, completing the healing of the family of faith.

"Why should we linger when Jesus is pleading, pleading for you and for me? Why should we wait, then, and heed not his mercies, mercies for you and for me? Come home, come home, ye who are weary, come home; earnestly, tenderly, Jesus is calling, calling, 'O sinner, come home!'"

CHAPTER 20

Loving
Eternally

A gay Christian wanted to test Jesus, so she asked, "Teacher, what do I have to do to live forever?" Jesus said, "What do you think?" She said, "Love God with all that you are and with all that you've got, and love your neighbor as much as you love yourself." Jesus answered, "That's right! Do this, and you will live."

But the gay Christian knew she didn't love God with all of her being and with all that she had, and that she didn't particularly *like* her neighbors, let alone love them. So she decided to ask another question, hoping somehow to get off the hook so she could still live forever: "Who is my neighbor? People like me? People with whom I agree? People who've helped me out?"

Jesus replied, "A person with AIDS was walking along the street when some hustlers began harassing him, taunting him about his KS lesions. They easily knocked him down in his weakened state, bloodying his nose in the fall.

"Two police officers drove by in a patrol car, but they were more interested in arresting prostitutes than coming to the aid of a downed person with AIDS. They also feared they might become infected were they to help.

"Then a gay Christian walked by, but since he was already late for a church committee meeting, he didn't take time to stop. He did offer a prayer for the PWA at the beginning of the meeting, however, and all the committee members lauded his sensitivity.

"But Jerry Falwell passed by in a limousine and saw the poor man. He ordered his driver to stop, went out to the man, helped him into his car, and took him to a first-class hotel, where he got him a room and had the hotel doctor look after his cuts and scrapes. Before he left the next morning, he paid the man's hotel bill, leaving additional money should he stay another night."

Jesus, having said this, asked the gay Christian, "Which of these three, do you think, proved neighbor to the person with AIDS harassed by hustlers?" The gay Christian replied reluctantly, "The one who showed mercy on him." And Jesus said, "Go and do likewise."

Jesus must have enjoyed shocking the self-righteous. We might protest, "But Jerry Falwell would never have stopped to help a person with AIDS!" When Jesus told this story about a Samaritan, hated and despised for racial and religious reasons, his listeners would have made a similar protest.

And Jesus didn't directly respond to the self-serving question of the lawyer who asked, "What shall I do to inherit eternal life?" "What is written in your law?" Jesus asked (Luke 18). The lawyer knew the summary of the law stated in both Leviticus and Deuteronomy about loving God with one's whole being and loving the neighbor as one's self. Nor did Jesus necessarily assure him of eternal life when he told him, "Do this, and you will live." The lawyer sensed this, and felt the need to justify himself. The lawyer was well acquainted with Jewish law which originally limited the concept of neighbor to fellow Jews. Later the definition of neighbor came to include foreigners who dwelt in their midst. But it certainly did not include Samaritans!

I believe that Jesus didn't always answer the questions he was asked because people were asking the wrong questions. He responded with questions, or parables, or answered a different question altogether. In this case, he did all three. Jesus doesn't answer the lawyer's first question about eternal life, but makes him answer it himself. Then, instead of answering the question, "Who is my neighbor?" he answers, "How does one serve as neighbor?" And Jesus illustrates the answer to this question with the parable of the Good Samaritan, who inconveniences himself and risks his own safety to care for a person beaten by robbers.

Personal immortality was an existential and theological topic of Jesus' day. Nearly two thousand years later, in the midst of great doubts about life beyond death, personal immortality of some kind is a common quest. The theme song of the movie *Fame* cried, "I want to live forever!" The hope expressed is not unlike that of the lawyer who questioned Jesus, "What shall I do to inherit eternal life?" The answer in the song is "fame," and the implication is that achievement will lead to a kind of immortality.

In Jane Chambers' magnificent play *Last Summer at Bluefish Cove*, a lesbian with a terminal illness is surrounded by other lesbian friends who have left their marks in life and have been guaranteed a type of personal immortality. One has written several books. Another has reared children. A third has accumulated wealth. The dying woman can point to no achievements, nothing she can leave behind. But ultimately she *does* leave behind something that is invaluable: her transformed lover, whom she has helped to own her feelings, to become independent, to care for herself. Her personal immortality is found in the gift of self-worth she has enabled her lover to discover. Her gift of compassion will live on.

Jesus seems to direct the lawyer to this kind of immortality in the parable of the Good Samaritan. It is not an immortality based in personal preservation, personal safety, or an extended quantity of life. Rather, it is an immortality based in risking one's life to find it, chancing even death, whether on a robber-infested road or on a God-forsaken cross, to enrich the quality of life for others.

The character of Chambers' play who lives on in our hearts is the woman who died of cancer, yet gave her lover new life. In Jesus' parable, the one who has lived on in its retelling was the victim of racial and religious bigotry. But victimization did not paralyze him from having compassion; perhaps it enabled a more passionate identification with others in need. For similar reasons, persons who have died of AIDS live on in our hearts, having given us insights into AIDS, into life, into death itself, enabling us to care for ourselves and one another. And most lesbian and gay Christians who fall victim to homophobia do not play the victim, preoccupied with ourselves, but stop to help the wounded of society who are ignored and abandoned by both society and church.

When I first heard the song "What I Did for Love" from the musical A Chorus Line, I believed the song described the investment of love between a couple or would-be couple that was breaking up. I thought of the many phone numbers exchanged, the glorious anticipation of first dates, the growing excitement that "this could be the one," the extraordinary measures and sacrifices to make it work, and the disappointment and deflation that came somewhere between the first date and the last when one or both people realized that this was not the one.

When I finally saw the musical on stage, I discovered the song's context. The character who sings it is describing a relationship to the theater, a chosen profession. The character had sacrificed everything for love of theater. Again, my heart recognized an experience and commitment identical in intensity to my own, though the object differed. As I reflected on "what I did for love" of the church, others in the audience probably reflected on what they had done for love of their professions and life pursuits.

A *Chorus Line* dramatizes the process of selecting actors for a Broadway show. In the anticipation of the winnowing out of the elect, the parabolic nature of the musical becomes clear. It is a story about human striving for everything from success in this life to heaven in the next. Within this context, "What I Did for Love" suggests that *all of life* is what we did for love. What's worth remembering in our lives *is* what we did for love. This was also Paul's conclusion: "So faith, hope, love abide, these three; but the greatest of these is love" (1 Cor. 13:13).

John the Baptist described Judgment Day as the separation of kernels of wheat from the chaff; the chaff is burned and the wheat saved. I believe that judgment is the burning of the chaff of our lives and that salvation is the saving of what is of value in our lives, what can grow and what may serve as nourishment for others; in other words, what we did for love. To paraphrase the song, love's what *God* remembers.

In my ten years of leading a Bible study for gay men and lesbian women, I have found that we have great difficulty with the theological doctrine of judgment. It is not surprising, given how much and how often we have been misjudged. It is helpful for us to remember that the Hebrew word for justice implies mercy and righteousness. God judges mercifully in a way the church has not. As Harry Emerson Fosdick once said about human vs. divine compassion, "God's at least as good as we are." In other words, if we would be forgiving toward someone, then surely God would be even more forgiving.

The Bible is the story of a God who comes down from the imposing mountain of requirements for choosing life (the Law of Moses given on Mount Sinai) to enter the depths of Sheol (as the Psalmist proclaims) by choosing death on a cross, to illustrate how far God will go to forgive and redeem humanity. From mountaintop to grave, the drama of the Bible describes what God did for love.

On the human side, however, many evil things have been done in the name of love: possessive love, conditional love, abusive love, crimes of passion, killing the neighbor for love of God or country, to give a few examples. In chapter 10 I recommended a definition of love from Scott Peck that I believe sums up the Christian view of love: "Love is the will to extend one's self for the purpose of nurturing one's own or another's spiritual growth."

As we judge our lives as individuals, as a church, and as a society, what we've done for this kind of love is what's worth remembering. This is what God remembers. God's saving grace is that, when it comes to our failures, inadequacies, mixed motives, and sins, God has a terrible memory. What we did for love is what God chooses to remember.

But what about evil? Will evil go unpunished? Will the Hitlers of our lives not burn in hell? If God remembers what we did for love, I believe that in the final reckoning, there will be some forgettable people. *And* there will be some forgettable pages and chapters of *our* lives that will burn in God's amnesiac fires. Only the heart of our life story, what we did for love, will be preserved.

Famed gay author Oscar Wilde wrote a wonderful children's story entitled *The Happy Prince.* The story begins, "High above the city, on a tall column, stood the statue of the Happy Prince. He was gilded all over with thin leaves of fine gold, for eyes he had two bright sapphires, and a large red ruby glowed on his swordhilt." The story describes how the Happy Prince whom the statue immortalized had lived in the palace years before, happily sheltered from the pain of the poor. Now, as a statue overlooking the city, he could easily witness all the poverty and suffering below. Though his heart was lead, tears welled up in his eyes.

A tear fell on a swallow at his feet, a swallow who then chose to love the statue, despite previous taunting from his fellow swallows for his queer affections. The Happy Prince persuaded the swallow to delay his trip south for the winter to run errands of compassion: taking the ruby from his sword-hilt to a poor seamstress with a sick son; delivering one of his sapphire eyes to a struggling writer who was hungry and cold; dropping off the other sapphire eye to a poor matchgirl whose father would beat her for not bringing money home; and peeling off the leaves of fine gold from the leaden statue to give to the poor.

By the time all this was done, winter had arrived, and it was too late for the swallow to fly south. The little bird died from the cold next to his beloved friend, the statue of the Happy Prince. The mayor and town councillors, noticing how shabby the statue had become, ordered it torn down and melted in a furnace. But the Happy Prince's broken lead heart would not melt, and so was cast onto a dustheap where the dead swallow was lying. The story ends: "'Bring me the two most precious things in the city,' said God to one of the Angels; and the Angel brought God the leaden heart and the dead bird. 'You have rightly chosen,' said God, 'For in my garden of Paradise this little bird shall sing for evermore, and in my city of gold the Happy Prince shall praise me.'"

So faith, hope, love abide, these three;
but the greatest of these is love.

Standing on the Threshold

In her "Spiritual Autobiography," contained in a letter to a priest, Simone Weil explained why, though a Christian, and though a catholic in the broad sense of the term, she chose not to join the Roman Catholic Church. "So many things are outside it," she wrote, "so many things that I love and do not want to give up, so many things that God loves, otherwise they would not be in existence." Finding herself at "the intersection of Christianity and everything that is not Christianity," she noted, "I have always remained at this exact point, on the threshold of the Church."[1]

Many lesbian and gay Christians stand with Simone Weil on the threshold of the church, some of us facing inward, some of us facing outward. We engage, confront, challenge, and even comfort the church by our very presence there, for we either have not run off with our inheritance or are returning. We are looking for some beckoning sign from the dysfunctional family within, dysfunctional in our experience because of its inability to talk about homosexuality.

One Christmas season, I attended a concert of the Los Angeles Gay Men's Chorus held in the cathedral-like sanctuary of the First United Methodist Church of Hollywood. Outside, "Jesus people" picketed the event, shouting chants that proclaimed the damnation of gays and lesbians. Inside,

211

their voices could be heard only during the silences between songs, carols sung by gay men about the miracle of God's grace manifest in Christ's nativity. Inside, the appreciative audience was gay and straight, multi-ethnic, families with children, lesbian and gay couples, single people.

I began to wonder where most Christians would place themselves in the scene. It occurred to me that most would not join those ranting outside. But I also believed that most would not yet feel comfortable hearing the gospel on the lips of gay men inside. Likely, I thought, most Christians would place themselves on the threshold of the church, unwilling to condemn us to hell, unwilling to embrace our own charism, our own special grace, our own unique gifts.

With all this imaging, first of lesbians and gays standing in the church's doorway, then of other Christians standing there, the threshold of the church is getting pretty crowded. Such a crush of intimacy, I believe, requires resolving our conflicts, if not our differences. Maybe we need to recognize that we are all prodigals and that we are all elder siblings. Maybe we all need to confess our sins as disobedient children, and, as loving parents, forgive one another. This will help us feel at home. It will enable us to make ourselves at home. We will be better able to help others feel at home.

And we may recognize that those of us standing on the threshold of the church are *also* the Church, at "the intersection of all that is Christianity and all that is not Christianity." We'll understand that the very fact that we can stand on the threshold implies that the door is open. And we'll remember Jesus' words: "I am the door; if any one enters by me, that one will be saved, and will go in and out and find pasture" (John 10:9). And we'll witness that Jesus is an open door through the walls of the closet, the church, and of death itself.

Then, I believe, our eyes will be opened and we will see that the Church itself is a threshold, one of many, that leads into the commonwealth of God. And we will see that we ourselves, as the Body of Christ, are standing in that doorway, beckoning yet others to come home.

Notes

CHAPTER 8. Developing Intimacy With God

1. Keating, Thomas, *Open Mind, Open Heart* (Amity, NY: Amity House, 1986).

CHAPTER 9. Rising Above Sin

1. Bornkamm, Günther, *Paul* (New York: Harper & Row, 1971), 133–34.

CHAPTER 10. Making Love

1. Peck, M. Scott, *The Road Less Travelled* (New York: Simon & Schuster, 1978), 81.

CHAPTER 11. Risking the Brokenness of the Body

1. Oberholtzer, Dwight, ed., *Is Gay Good?* (Philadelphia: Westminster Press, 1972), 204–12.
2. Hartshorne, Charles, *The Divine Relativity* (New Haven: Yale University Press, 1969).

CHAPTER 13. Turning the Church Upside Down

1. Peck, M. Scott, *People of the Lie: The Hope for Healing Human Evil* (New York: Simon & Schuster, 1983), especially chapter 6.

CHAPTER 16. Evangelizing

1. Leith, John H., *Introduction to the Reformed Tradition* (Atlanta: John Knox Press, 1977), 69.

CHAPTER 17. Making the World Safe for Diversity

1. Hillesum, Etty, *An Interrupted Life* (New York: Washington Square Press, Simon & Schuster, 1983), 89, 159, 190, 217.

CHAPTER 19. Healing AIDS

1. Weber, Hans-Ruedi, ed., *On a Friday Noon* (Geneva: World Council of Churches; Grand Rapids, MI: Eerdmans, 1979), 18.
2. Bonhoeffer, Dietrich, *Life Together* (New York: Harper & Row, 1954), chapters 1 and 3.

Epilogue. Standing on the Threshold

1. Panichas, George A., ed., *Simone Weil Reader* (Mt. Kisco, NY: Moyer Bell Limited, 1977), 20, 21.